BACK TO SCHOOL

1,001 FACTS

YOU LEARNED

AND FORGOT —IN—

HIGH SCHOOL

BENJAMIN SMITH

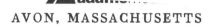

AVON, MASSACHUSETTS

Published by
Adams Media, a division of F+W Media, Inc.
57 Littlefield Street, Avon, MA 02322. U.S.A.
www.adamsmedia.com

Contains material adapted and abridged from *The Lazy Intellectual* by Richard J. Wallace and James V. Wallace, copyright © 2010 by F+W Media, Inc., ISBN 10: 1-4405-0456-3, ISBN 13: 978-1-4405-0456-3; *A Ton of Crap* by Paul Kleinman, copyright © 2011 by F+W Media, Inc., ISBN 10: 1-4405-2935-3, ISBN 13: 978-1-4405-2935-1; *The Everything® Kids' Geography Book* by Jane P. Gardner and J. Elizabeth Mills, copyright © 2009 by F+W Media, Inc., ISBN 10: 1-59869-683-1, ISBN 13: 978-1-59869-683-7; *The Everything® Kids' Soccer Book, 2nd Edition* by Deborah Crisfield, copyright © 2009, 2002 by F+W Media, Inc., ISBN 10: 1-60550-162-X, ISBN 13: 978-1-60550-162-8; *The Everything® Guide to Calculus I* by Greg Hill, copyright © 2011 by F+W Media, Inc., ISBN 10: 1-4405-0629-9, ISBN 13: 978-1-4405-0629-1; *The Bullsh*t Artist* by Paul Kleinman, copyright © 2011 by F+W Media, Inc., ISBN 10: 1-4405-1255-8, ISBN 13: 978-1-4405-1255-1.

ISBN 10: 1-4405-8598-9
ISBN 13: 978-1-4405-8598-2
eISBN 10: 1-4405-8599-7
eISBN 13: 978-1-4405-8599-9

Printed in the United States of America.

10   9   8   7   6   5   4   3   2   1

Cover design by Frank Rivera.
Cover images © tindo/Goce Risteski/Michael Travers/123RF; Clipart.com.

This book is available at quantity discounts for bulk purchases.
For information, please call 1-800-289-0963.

CLASS SCHEDULE

INTRODUCTION

ATTENTION, ALL STUDENTS. This is your principal here. It's been a long time since you walked down these halls, and sat at these tiny desks, but the time has come to get schooled once again. What happened to all of the biology, geometry, ancient history, and foreign languages that you learned here all those years ago? That's what we'd all like to know.

By re-enrolling, you're admitting that you've forgotten almost as much as you learned back in high school, but you're also admitting that some of this stuff might actually be useful to know. (If your sixteen-year-old self could only see you now.) Over the course of these lessons, we'll try to fill your head with as much knowledge as we can cram in there, but this time it's going to stick. Sure, photosynthesis, and the Cold War, and the prepositional phrases don't come up a lot in everyday conversation, but when they do, do you want to be able to contribute to thoughtful conversation? The choice is yours.

This book gives you a chance to redo ten of your favorite courses from your high-school days without having to deal with prom queens and jocks or stoners and bullies. From geography to literature, and philosophy to phys. ed., you'll learn all the most useful facts you thought were long forgotten, and maybe a few things you never knew in the first place.

Just remember a few school rules: no cheating, no gum-chewing, and no texting in class. While you're here, feel free to join some extracurriculars, but just remember to study up, because there will be a final exam. So grab your pencil and your notebook, because it's time to go back to school.

The bell is about to ring, so head straight to first period, and don't be late.

PERIOD 1
ENGLISH

READING AND WRITING ARE PERHAPS THE MOST IMPORTANT SKILLS you will take from high school to adulthood. If you can't communicate properly, it will be difficult to succeed at whatever career you choose. This class will be a refresher course in proper grammar and writing skills, followed by a whistle-stop tour of English and American literature. When someone asks you your favorite book at a dinner party, this might just give you a few to choose from.

FRESHMAN YEAR: LANGUAGE ARTS

PUNCTUATION

Use of **PUNCTUATION** dates back to ancient Greece and Rome. Orators placed marks in their speeches to indicate where and when to pause. These marks were given names such as period, comma, and colon, correlating to the kind of pauses needed. Punctuation was used infrequently, and it was not until the fifteenth century, with the introduction and rise of printing in England, that the punctuation we know today began to be used.

∽

A **PERIOD** is used at the end of a sentence to create a statement and complete a thought. A period can also be used at the end of a command, such as, "When you've finished the last part of the exam, put your pencils down." A period is also used to end an indirect question, for example, "Her boss asked her why she didn't come to work on Monday."

∽

The **COMMA** has many uses. A comma should be used to separate any independent clause joined by the conjunctions *and, yet, so, but, for, nor,* and *or.* A comma is also used to separate items in a list or series and after an introductory adverb clause. The comma can also be used to interrupt a sentence to add extra information. For example, "Her dog, which had jumped in the puddle, was soaking wet."

∽

As a general rule you can use a **SEMICOLON** instead of a period to connect two sentences without a conjunction. For example, "Give me your number; I'll call you when I get home." A semicolon should also be used before transitional adverbs like *however, therefore,* and *namely.* One can also use a semicolon in a series if one or more of the items includes a comma, or when two sentences are joined by a coordinating conjunction and there are commas in the first sentence.

EXTRACURRICULARS: NEWSPAPER
OXFORD COMMA SPURS CONTROVERSY

The **OXFORD COMMA**, also known as the serial comma or the Harvard comma, may be punctuation's most controversial mark. It is used immediately before a coordinating conjunction (usually *and, or, nor*) in a list of items. Some reference books, like the *MLA Style Manual and Guide to Scholarly Publishing* and *The Chicago Manual of Style* demand its use, while *The Associated Press Stylebook* and *The Canadian Press Stylebook* are firmly against it. Those opposed find it redundant, and those in favor feel it resolves ambiguity.

ఐ

A **COLON** is used if one wishes to emphasize the second of two independent clauses. For example, "The time had passed: his date never showed up." A colon can also be used to introduce a list, a quotation, an appositive (in which two phrases are placed next to each other, with one serving to define or change the other), or another idea related to the independent clause.

ఐ

An **EM DASH** is used to place emphasis on or set content apart from the rest of the text. Named because it is the width of an *M*, this dash is longer and places more importance on text than parentheses do. For example, "A lot of people were in the crowd—Tom and Scott among them." The **EN DASH**, which is the width of an *N*, is shorter and is used to indicate a span of values between two numbers. For example, "For ages 3–5."

SENTENCE COMPOSITION

Knowledge of **PARTS OF SPEECH**, or word classes, is critical in understanding how composition works. Parts of speech are **NOUNS**, (people, places, or things); **PRONOUNS** (words like *he*, *she*, and *it* used to replace nouns); **ADJECTIVES** (words that describe nouns); **VERBS** (actions); **ADVERBS** (words that modify adjectives, verbs, other adverbs, or an entire clause or sentence by expressing place, manner, or time); **CONJUNCTIONS** (words used to connect phrases or sentences such as *and*, *but*, and *because*); **ARTICLES** (words that indicate nouns and specify their application, such as *a*, *an*, and *the*); **PREPOSITIONS** (words like *at*, *by*, *with*, and *from* used to link nouns, pronouns, or phrases to other parts of the sentence); and **INTERJEC-TIONS** (words that show emotion and are capable of standing alone, like *wow*, or *ugh*.)

∽

The three main parts of a sentence are the subject, the verb, and often, the object. The **SUBJECT** is usually the noun, and it is who or what the sentence is about. The **VERB** then follows the subject, indicating what action takes place. Lastly, the **OBJECT** follows the verb and is what receives the action. In the sentence "Tom threw the ball to Sally," *Tom* is the subject because the sentence is about him. The action, *threw*, is the verb, and *Sally* is the object, the receiver of Tom's action.

∽

A **MODIFIER** is any word, clause, or phrase that adds meaning to another word or part of a sentence. There are two types of modifiers, premodifiers and postmodifiers. The head is any word that will be modified. A premodifier goes before the head, as in "A history book," and a postmodifier appears after the head, for example, "A book about history."

∽

A **PREPOSITIONAL PHRASE** adds meaning to the verbs and nouns in a sentence. It is composed of two parts: a preposition (a word that expresses how a noun or pronoun relates to other words in the sentence), and the object of the preposition. For example, when looking at the phrase "In the building," the word *in* is our preposition because it indicates the relationship, and *the building* is the object of the preposition. Some other examples of prepositions include *above*, *between*, *inside*, *up*, *down*, and *through*.

∽

ADJECTIVE CLAUSES help indicate which part of a sentence is more important than the rest of the sentence by a process known as subordination. The adjective clause is a dependent word group that modifies the noun and usually includes words like *which*, *who*, *whose*, and *that*. In the sentence, "The dog that ate everyone's lunch wanted seconds," *that ate everyone's lunch* is the adjective clause.

∽

A **PARTICIPLE** is a verb form that is used as an adjective. For example, *cooked*, *cooking*, and *having cooked* are participles of the verb *cook*. A participle phrase is a sentence that consists of a present or past participle, with any modifiers, objects, and complements. In the example, "Running down the aisle, she knocked over the soup display," *running down the aisle* is the participle phrase.

FIGURES OF SPEECH

A **FIGURE OF SPEECH** is a literary device used to add interest, emphasis, freshness, or special meaning to words. A figure of speech can also be referred to as a rhetorical device or locution. Figures of speech are used in figurative (meaning not literal) language, allowing for imagination and more creative ways to describe something.

∽

A **SIMILE** is one of the most common figures of speech. In similes, one thing is described to be like another thing. The important part about similes is their use of the word *like* or *as*. For example, "He eats like a pig" and "It's as light as a feather" are both similes. Other forms of simile can be found in sentences with *as if* and *than*. Two examples are, "I completely forgot how to work the machine, as if it was my very first time," and "Larger than life."

∽

METAPHORS are very similar to similes, only they do not use *like*, *as*, *as if*, or *than*. Instead, they simply state that one thing *is* another thing. In the sentence, "Her home is a pigsty," we understand that this does not mean her home is a literal pigsty, but rather a very messy place. A metaphor and simile can mean the same thing, but they are worded differently. "He is a snake" is a metaphor. "He is like a snake" is a simile.

∽

HYPERBOLE is a form of exaggeration used to elicit a strong response. Hyperboles are not to be taken literally and are often used for humor. For example, "He is older than the dinosaurs," and "I'm a million times smarter than you," are both hyperboles. There is great exaggeration in these sentences. Hyperbole is very common in media and advertising.

An **OXYMORON** pairs two opposite or contradicting ideas to create a new meaning or paradoxical image. For example, "bittersweet chocolate." *Bitter* and *sweet* are opposites, and yet when put together, they take on a whole new meaning. Other examples of oxymora include *deafening silence, jumbo shrimp,* and *freezer burn.*

Other common examples of figures of speech include **ALLITERATION**, where there is a repetition of the beginning consonant; **ANAPHORA**, the repetition of a single word or phrase at the beginning of successive phrases or paragraphs; **ONOMATOPOEIA**, the use of words that imitate the sounds they are referring to; and **ANTITHESIS**, which juxtaposes opposite ideas in a single, balanced sentence.

THE PARAGRAPH

A **PARAGRAPH** is a group of sentences that are related in the subject they are discussing. Good paragraphs are crucial to being a good writer or just having your writing make sense to the reader. Paragraphs organize sentences so that the main idea can get across in an easy and coherent way. A good rule of thumb to follow is to always keep one idea for every paragraph.

The **TOPIC SENTENCE** tells the reader what the rest of the paragraph will be about. Though the topic sentence does not need to be the very first sentence in the paragraph, it certainly is a good approach to take. The idea is that one would be able to summarize from the topic sentence what that paragraph is about. The sentence doesn't have to blatantly state the topic at the beginning, as long as the paragraph is understandable.

∽

SUPPORTING SENTENCES do just that; they support. If the topic sentence is the main idea of the paragraph, then the supporting sentences should provide the necessary information (images, data, analysis) to back up that statement. A good rule of thumb when writing paragraphs is they should be five to seven sentences long. That should provide enough support for the main idea you are trying to get across.

∽

The **CONCLUDING SENTENCE** is kind of like the reverse of the topic sentence. Instead of beginning a topic for discussion, this is meant to conclude the main idea of the paragraph. One type of concluding sentence would be to summarize all that was said in the topic sentence and supporting sentences. Not every paragraph needs a concluding sentence, but if the paragraph is long or has lots of information, a concluding sentence can be very useful.

∽

It can be hard to know when a paragraph has enough information or perhaps too little information. To make sure your paragraph is well developed, here are some helpful tips: Make sure you describe the topic you're going to talk about, then analyze and cite any information that supports it. Include facts and details, talk about causes and effects, use stories or anecdotes, define terms, and compare and contrast when you can.

∽

There are a couple of ways to know when you need to start a new paragraph. The most obvious is when you begin discussing a new topic or a new idea. Similarly, if the material contrasts the material before it, you should begin a new paragraph. Even if your idea is continuing, however, a paragraph that goes on for too long can become hard to read. Start a new paragraph to give the reader's eyes a break. Lastly, you want new paragraphs to begin your introduction and your conclusion.

EDITING

Editing and proofreading are not interchangeable. Both are very important to the process of good writing. **EDITING** is about making sure language is used correctly. It's about ensuring that every term that is used is the correct term, and often includes research. **PROOFREADING** is a final check of your writing to make sure that everything is grammatically sound and that there are no syntax or spelling errors.

∽

Once your writing is finished, it is absolutely necessary that you go back and edit. Your first draft should never be your final draft. Think about your audience. Who are you writing this for? Is it a technical audience? Do you need to explain any technical terms or will they understand what you're talking about? How old is your audience? Children have a shorter attention span than adults. Think about the length of your sentences. Make sure what you have written is appropriate for your readers.

∽

Once you have made any changes that are needed, your last step is to proofread. There are several methods of proofreading. First, be aware of your strengths and weaknesses. If punctuation is not your strong suit, make sure to check every sentence for punctuation errors. One very effective way to proofread is to read what you've written from bottom to top and from right to left. By doing this, mistakes will stick out like a sore thumb. You should also scan your paper all the way through for any typos. Reading your writing out loud will also give new insights and help you spot any errors.

SOPHOMORE YEAR: LITERATURE & POETRY

LITERARY TERMS

In literature, **GENRE** refers to a specific category marked by a distinctive style, form, or content. It is instantly recognizable and follows common conventions pertaining to that genre. Examples of genres include **NONFICTION**, in which everything written is true; **MYSTERY**, a fictional story that follows and solves a crime; and **FANTASY**, which features elements that are not realistic.

∽

An **ALLEGORY** is a narrative that is symbolic of something else. With allegories, behind the literal translation of the story, a second, more meaningful story or idea can be found. For example, the literal story of *Lord of the Flies* is about children stranded on an island where chaos ensues; however, the allegory is about civilization as a whole and the evil of humankind.

∽

CATHARSIS is a point in the narrative when there is a release of negative emotions, which in turn ends up either helping the character or helping the audience understand the character. The term comes from the Greek *katharsis* which means "purification" or "cleansing."

The term was first applied to literature in Aristotle's *Poetics*, in which he describes the impact of drama on an audience.

∽

AMBIGUITY allows room for different interpretations of a work of literature by creating an openness in the text. Ambiguity is sometimes considered a flaw, a lack of detail or vague characterization; however, it can also be used purposefully and skillfully to the advantage of the story.

∽

METANOIA, which comes from the Greek *metanoiein*, meaning "to change one's mind," is a rhetorical device that an author uses to retract a statement and then state it better. It can be used to either weaken or strengthen the original statement, depending on the context.

∽

A **MOTIF** is a recurring image, phrase, element, expression, word, action, or object that has some sort of symbolic significance to the story. Motifs can help develop the theme of the narrative. A motif can also refer to a situation, character, image, idea, or incident found in literature. For example, a love triangle and the corruption of power are motifs.

EXTRACURRICULARS: DRAMA CLUB
WICKED: THE LIFE AND TIMES OF THE WICKED WITCH OF THE WEST is a bestselling novel written by Gregory Maguire. It was conceived as a prequel to L. Frank Baum's children's novel, **THE WONDERFUL WIZARD OZ**, and tells the story of the misunderstood Wicked Witch of the West. In 2003 it was adapted for Broadway, and has become one of the most successful musicals of all time.

PARTS OF A STORY

Simply put, the **PLOT** is the story found in literature, film, television, or other narrative work. It is the sequence of events that make up the story. German novelist Gustav Freytag considered the plot to any story to be composed of five parts: exposition, which introduces the main characters and their stories and relationships; a rising action, which begins with a conflict of some sort (this generally involves the character striving for a certain goal); the climax, which is the turning point of the story; the falling action, where loose ends are tied up; and lastly, the resolution or denouement.

∽

The **PROTAGONIST** is the main character of the story, the character who drives the plot of the story. For example, even though in *The Wizard of Oz* the plot is about finding the Wizard, the story's protagonist is actually Dorothy, because the story is about her journey, not the Wizard. The protagonist can sometimes be the narrator of the story. A **FALSE PROTAGONIST** is a dramatic device where the protagonist is disposed of unexpectedly. A famous example of this is Hitchcock's *Psycho*, where the main character is killed halfway through the movie.

∽

The **ANTAGONIST** is the character in opposition to the protagonist. The antagonist may also represent a threat or opposing idea to the protagonist. For example, if the superhero is the protagonist, the evil villain is the antagonist. A classic example of an antagonist is Voldemort or Snape from the Harry Potter series. Harry is the protagonist, and they are his antagonists.

FORESHADOWING is used to hint at developments that will occur later on in the plot. Formal patterning is a form of foreshadowing where certain events, actions, and gestures let the reader anticipate the plot. A red herring is a hint dropped into a story to intentionally mislead the reader.

POINT OF VIEW is the perspective from which the story is being told. A narrator can tell the story in first person, from the narrator's experience of events (uses the pronoun *I*). This point of view is limited to the information the narrator can directly know or observe. The third-person narrator is an offstage, unnamed observer who is not part of the story itself (uses pronouns *he* and *she*). An omniscient narrator can relate multiple characters' perspectives, moving freely in and out of all the characters' thoughts. A limited omniscient narrator is confined to the thoughts of one character at a time. Both omniscient and limited omniscient narrators are examples of third-person narration.

The **SETTING** of a story is more than just a backdrop for the actions to occur. It also sets the mood and tone of the entire story, as well as any context that needs to be understood. The setting establishes the time period, the culture, and the geography, and in some cases the setting can be just as important as the characters.

POETRY

NARRATIVE POETRY is like a story because it has a plot, but it is told in verse form and includes epic poems, ballads, and idylls. Narrative poems can be long or short, intricate and complex, or simple. They usually are nondramatic and have a regular meter. One example of a narrative poem is *The Canterbury Tales* by Geoffrey Chaucer.

෴

EPIC POEMS are longer narrative poems, and usually center on a hero and his heroic journey and deeds. Epic poetry has its history in the oral tradition, and has been recorded since the time of the ancient Greeks. One of the most famous epic poems ever written is *The Odyssey* by Homer, which follows Odysseus's journey back home following the Trojan War.

෴

One of the most common forms of poetry is the **SONNET**, perhaps most famously written by William Shakespeare. Sonnets must be fourteen lines and written in iambic pentameter with one of the various rhyme schemes. The first quatrain of the poem must be expositional and discuss the main theme and metaphor. The second quatrain complicates or extends the theme. The third quatrain introduces a twist, and then finally the couplet summarizes the poem, leaving the reader with a new image to end on.

෴

RHYTHM, also known as measure, is the equivalent of beat in music. In poetry, certain words may be held longer or pronounced with more force than other words. A rhythmic effect is produced from this pattern of emphasis. Sometimes rhythm is obvious, but rhythm can also be more muted and subtle.

෴

METER is the recurring pattern of stressed and unstressed syllables in lines of verse. For example, if a line of poetry contains fifteen syllables, the first syllable is unstressed, the second stressed, the next unstressed, and so on. A foot is a set combination of unstressed and stressed syllables. Different meters are used for different types of poetry. Iambic meter has unstressed and then stressed syllables, while dactylic has a stressed syllable followed by two unstressed syllables.

ທ

A **STANZA** is two or more lines of a poem that together form one of the divisions. Stanzas are usually the same length and follow the same pattern of meter and rhyme. Couplets are stanzas that have two lines, usually rhyme, and often form a complete thought. Tercets are composed of three lines of poetry which may or may not rhyme. If they rhyme they are called triplets. Quatrains have four lines and are written in any type of rhyme scheme.

JUNIOR YEAR: ENGLISH LITERATURE

SHAKESPEARE

WILLIAM SHAKESPEARE lived from 1564 to 1616 in England. Very little is known of his childhood, including the date of his actual birth. Shakespeare did not attend university when he got older, which was reserved for the wealthy, and by the time he was eighteen years old in 1582, he was married. By 1585 Shakespeare, had moved to London to pursue acting and playwriting. He wrote his first play, *Henry VI, Part I*, during the early 1590s, and thereafter became a popular playwright. In 1593, his poem *Venus and Adonis* was published and achieved great success.

Shakespeare wrote some of the world's most famous comedies, tragedies, and histories, as well as sonnets and poems. The general consensus is that he wrote a total of thirty-seven plays; however, others believe that including possible lost works and collaborations, it's really more like forty. He also wrote 154 sonnets and two long-form narrative poems.

His most famous plays include:

- *Romeo and Juliet*
- *Hamlet*
- *Othello*
- *Macbeth*
- *King Lear*
- *A Midsummer Night's Dream*

Shakespeare's plays feature blank verse, lines of **IAMBIC PENTAMETER** that do not rhyme. When passages deviated within the plays, Shakespeare would use a different poetic form or simple prose. With one exception, all his sonnets are written in iambic pentameter.

Shakespeare also invented words and phrases (at least 1,500 credited to him). Among the many words he invented or made popular are *assassination, bump, submerge, frugal, gnarled, dishearten, obscene, generous,* and *monumental.*

Shakespeare's best-known plays were performed at the **GLOBE THEATRE** in London. The theater was built by the brother of Richard Burbage, one of the actors who worked with Shakespeare, who wrote for the troupe. From 1592 to 1593, an outbreak of the plague caused the theater to shut down, and it is during this time that William Shakespeare turned to poetry. In 1594, the Globe Theatre reopened, and Shakespeare and the troupe became extremely popular. The Globe Theatre could seat two to three thousand people, and performances were held in the afternoon to take advantage of daylight. During a performance of *Henry VIII* on June 29, 1613, a cannon was fired and it set the roof on fire, burning the Globe Theatre to the ground.

Since the 1700s, there have been various people, known as **ANTI-STRATFORDIANS**, questioning whether William Shakespeare actually wrote all of his plays or whether they were written by his contemporaries. There are three main candidates believed to have authored the plays Shakespeare takes credit for: Edward de Vere, Francis Bacon, and Christopher Marlowe. Edward de Vere, 17th Earl of Oxford, was a nobleman of Queen Elizabeth I, and many believe his life resembled content found in Shakespeare's plays. Perhaps the strongest candidate is Francis Bacon, whose book *Promus of Formularies and Elegancies* features 4,400 parallels in terms of thought and expression. Christopher Marlowe was a playwright who was stabbed to death in a bar fight in 1593. Some believe he was actually a spy who faked his own death and continued to write plays under the pen name William Shakespeare.

VICTORIAN LITERATURE

The **VICTORIAN ERA** is the transitional period between the romantic period and the twentieth century, during the reign of Queen Victoria in Britain (1837–1901). Literature produced during this time dealt with the issues of daily life. With the rise of industrialism, reform movements involving child labor, women's rights, emancipation, and the concept of evolution heavily influenced the work, and the Victorian era is considered to be one of pessimism and doubt. Literature had a moral purpose, and featured ideals like love, justice, and truth.

∞

During the nineteenth century, the **NOVEL** became the most popular form of literature. Novels focused on portraying the difficulty of real life, in which ultimately it is love, perseverance, and hard work that win out. An especially important part of the novel during this time was the depiction of the emerging and expanding middle class, a departure from the aristocratic portrayals found in earlier novels. Most of the novels were published serially in journals, the latest chapter or section appearing with each new issue and featuring intricate plots and plot twists to keep readers interested.

∞

The most highly regarded poet during the Victorian era was **ALFRED, LORD TENNYSON**. His poetry reflected the feelings of the era, expressing melancholy and doubts about religion, yet confidence in class. There was a movement in the middle of the nineteenth century known as the Pre-Raphaelite movement that focused on reviving the work of medieval and classical times. The greatest example of this movement can be found in Tennyson's *Idylls of the King*, which combines the story of King Arthur with ideas and issues of the modern day.

∞

The Victorian era can be divided into three parts: the early Victorian period (which ended around 1848), the mid period (from 1848 until 1870), and the late Victorian period (which lasted from 1870 to 1901). In the late Victorian period, the principles that followed throughout the Victorian era were rejected. There was a return to fantasy, with such works as Robert Louis Stevenson's *The Strange Case of Dr. Jekyll and Mr. Hyde*, and the emergence of the "problem novel."

Problem novels focus on the institution of marriage and the role of the sexes and sexual identity.

ↄ

Children's literature changed during the Victorian era. By 1848, the work of Hans Christian Andersen was translated into English, sparking a great interest in fairy tales. It is during the Victorian era, for example, that Lewis Carroll's *Alice's Adventures in Wonderland* came out and became popular. The change in children's literature was the direct result of a time period when views on children began to shift. Child labor and required education of children came to the forefront of social issues. As more children began reading, an industry based on producing literature for them began to grow.

THREE FAMOUS ENGLISH AUTHORS

JANE AUSTEN was born on December 16, 1775, in Hampshire, England, and by 1787, Jane began writing plays, poetry, and stories. Her sense of humor was evident from the beginning, and she keenly watched the interactions of the social classes. Jane Austen's work is known for its realism, humor, and social commentary.

ↄ

NOTABLE JANE AUSTEN WORKS:

- *SENSE AND SENSIBILITY* was Jane Austen's first published novel. The book came out in 1811, and Austen credited herself with the pseudonym "A Lady." Jane Austen would continue to publish anonymously until the day she died, with only her family knowing it was she who was writing the books. The book follows two sisters who relocate to a new home after their father's death and experience romance and heartbreak. The book sold out all 750 copies in its first edition.

- **PRIDE AND PREJUDICE** was published in 1813. The book, like much of Austen's work, uses free indirect speech (meaning in the third person with the essence of first person) to tell the story. The book focuses on the importance of one's environment and how it affects upbringing, and that wealth and high social status do not necessarily confer advantage.
- **EMMA** was published in December of 1815. Once again, the book focuses on misconstrued romance among genteel women. Before writing the novel, Austen said, "I am going to take a heroine whom no one but myself will much like." Emma is a spoiled woman who overestimates her matchmaking abilities. Emma is the first heroine of any of Austen's books who does not have financial problems, and Emma is a major shift away from earlier themes in Austen's work, such as finding a husband and financial security.

ᨀ

CHARLES DICKENS is one of the Victorian era's best-known writers. Dickens' work focuses on hypocrisy, injustice, and social evils, and much of his work draws upon his actual life and features comic characters and social commentary. Dickens lived from 1812 to 1870. Like other Victorian works, his writing was often serialized, and in total, Dickens wrote fifteen novels. Dickens began his career as a journalist at the age of sixteen, and he continued working in journalism for the rest of his life.

ᨀ

NOTABLE CHARLES DICKENS WORKS:

- **A CHRISTMAS CAROL:** Though Dickens's *A Christmas Carol* is a celebration of Christmas, at its heart the novel is a social commentary on the division of the rich and poor in Victorian England. At the time of its writing, the British government enforced what were known as the English Poor Laws, which made the poor labor in horrible factories and live in debtor's prisons. When Dickens was twelve years old, his own family was moved to a debtor's prison, and Dickens was forced to work in a shoe polish factory.

- **_DAVID COPPERFIELD_**: Charles Dickens's eighth novel was _David Copperfield_, published in 1849. The book is considered the closest Charles Dickens ever came to writing an autobiography. In July of 1948, Dickens's sister, the model for Scrooge's sister Fan in _A Christmas Carol_, became terminally ill and died in September. Dickens intended to write an autobiography, but the process proved too painful for him, so instead, he invented a character and told his story through David Copperfield, whose initials are the inverse of Charles Dickens. In the book, many of the events portrayed are dramatizations of Dickens's life.
- **_A TALE OF TWO CITIES_**: Published in 1859, Dickens's twelfth novel, _A Tale of Two Cities_, was a departure in many ways for the author. The story is historical, against the backdrop of the French Revolution, and is less character-driven than focused on political events. Dickens shows both the cruelty of the French aristocracy and the suffering of the poor, justifying the need to revolt, but he also depicts the heinous deeds of those revolutionaries as they come to power.

∽

Born Adeline Virginia Stephen in 1882, **VIRGINIA WOOLF** was educated at home by her father, founding editor of the _Dictionary of English Biography_. Woolf suffered from depression and severe mental illness all her life. Her first of a series of nervous breakdowns began after her mother's death when she was just thirteen. When her father died in 1904, she had to be hospitalized. Her writing is considered to be some of the best feminist and modernist work.

NOTABLE VIRGINIA WOOLF WORKS:

- ***THE VOYAGE OUT***: Virginia Woolf's first published novel. The book was written at a time when Virginia was struggling with serious depression; she attempted suicide at least once during the process. Her feelings of domestic repression and the impact of the Bloomsbury Group can be found in the book. *The Voyage Out* also contains the beginnings of a focus on sexuality, female consciousness, and death, themes that would later become prevalent in her work.

- ***MRS. DALLOWAY***: One of Virginia Woolf's most well-regarded novels is *Mrs. Dalloway*, published in 1925. The book examines a single day in the life of a woman, Clarissa Dalloway, in post–World War I England. The narrative structure jumps in and out of the character's mind and forward and back in time. The book features themes of mental illness, depression, homosexuality, feminism, and existential issues.

- ***TO THE LIGHTHOUSE***: It is considered to be Virginia Woolf's greatest work and a modernist masterpiece. The structure of the narrative is less centered on plot and more focused on character introspection and consciousness. There is no outside narrator in the story, but rather the story is told by shifting from one consciousness to another. The existence of God is discussed and questioned.

EXTRACURRICULARS: YEARBOOK
MOST LIKELY TO BE RICHER THAN THE QUEEN
J.K. ROWLING wrote the first **HARRY POTTER** book while she was on Britain's version of welfare. Though it was initially rejected by a number of publishers, eventually it was published, and seven books later became one of the greatest literary phenomena of all time.

SENIOR YEAR: AMERICAN LITERATURE

EARLY AMERICAN LITERATURE

THE POWER OF SYMPATHY, written by William Hill Brown and published in 1789 in Boston, is considered the first American novel. It's a morality tale about the danger of seduction.

☙

The bestselling book of the nineteenth century was ***CHARLOTTE TEMPLE*** by Susanna Rowson. It was first published in 1791 in London, and reissued in the United States in 1794. It is another tale of seduction, which was a popular theme in early American novels.

☙

In 1852, Harriet Beecher Stowe's ***UNCLE TOM'S CABIN*** became the new bestseller, and was the most popular novel of the time. The book depicts the realities of slavery and is said to have laid the groundwork for the Civil War.

☙

RALPH WALDO EMERSON and **HENRY DAVID THOREAU** are known for forming the **TRANSCENDENTALISM** movement, which believed that society and institutions corrupted the individual, and looked back toward the natural world. Thoreau's ***WALDEN*** is a memoir about giving up on society and living alone in the woods for two years.

EDGAR ALLAN POE

EDGAR ALLAN POE was born on January 19, 1809, in Boston, Massachusetts. Poe's mother left his father and took the children with her. When Poe was only two years old, his mother died and Edgar was taken in by Frances and John Allan. Poe spent five years studying in England, and in 1826, he attended the University of Virginia. Less than a year later, Poe quit school due to drinking and heavy debt. The next year, he joined the army. By 1835, Poe was living in Baltimore, working as an editor of a newspaper. In 1836, Poe married his thirteen-year-old cousin and moved to New York City. In 1847, his wife died of tuberculosis two years after *The Raven* was published.

ⰰ

Poe's writing belongs to what is known as the **AMERICAN ROMANTIC MOVEMENT**. Literature of American romanticism focused on nature, the power of one's imagination, and individuality. Poe's life was dark and extremely emotional, and his poetry reflected this. His work featured mystical, magical, and mysterious elements in ways that set his work apart from realism. Other writers of American romanticism include Henry David Thoreau, Walt Whitman, Emily Dickinson, Washington Irving, and Herman Melville.

ⰰ

THE RAVEN, arguably Edgar Allan Poe's most famous poem, was first published on January 29, 1845, in the New York *Evening Mirror* to rave reviews. The poem tells the story of a man who desires his love who has died. He is visited by a talking bird that only says one word: "Nevermore." The man, so caught up in his imagination, believes the bird is telling him that he will never be reunited with his love. Poe said *The Raven* discusses man's proclivity to torture himself.

It is unknown what caused Edgar Allan Poe's death. What is known is that Poe died on October 7, 1849, in Baltimore. Days earlier, he was discovered outside of a bar, lying on a wooden plank, and was taken to the hospital. Records of his hospitalization indicate that he was delirious, hallucinating, and having tremors until he ultimately slipped into a coma. When he came out of the coma, he was at first calm, but then became increasingly delirious and combative. Four days later, he died. The cause of death on his death certificate reads "congestion of the brain." Many believed this to be alcohol related; however, Poe had not had any alcohol six months prior to his death. Researchers today believe the cause of death was rabies.

> **EXTRACURRICULARS: STUDENT COUNCIL**
> Norman Mailer, the Pulitzer Prize–winning author of *The Executioner's Song*, ran unsuccessfully for mayor of New York City in 1969.

FAMOUS AMERICAN AUTHORS

NATHANIEL HAWTHORNE was born July 4, 1804 in Salem, Massachusetts. He added the *w* to his last name so that he would not be associated with his ancestor, John Hathorne, a judge in the Salem witch trials. He published his first novel in 1821, and continued to write until his death in 1864. His works mostly take place in New England and many feature moral allegories.

∽

NOTABLE NATHANIEL HAWTHORNE WORKS:

- ***THE SCARLET LETTER***: Considered to be his most important work, *The Scarlet Letter* was published in 1850, and takes place in

Boston during the seventeenth century. The novel tells the story of Hester Prynne, who tries to re-establish her life and her dignity after an adulterous affair.

- **THE HOUSE OF THE SEVEN GABLES:** Published in 1851, *The House of the Seven Gables* follows a New England family, the Pyncheons, in their home in Salem, Massachusetts. The title was inspired by a real home with seven gables, open today as a museum.

৩

LOUISA MAY ALCOTT, born in 1832, was raised by transcendentalist parents in New England. She found success as a writer starting in 1860, and is best known for her Little Women series.

৩

NOTABLE LOUISA MAY ALCOTT WORKS:

- **LITTLE WOMEN:** Originally published in two volumes in 1868 and 1869, *Little Women* follows the lives of the four March sisters— Meg, Jo, Amy, and Beth. The story has become one of the most timeless in American literature, and has been made into several successful Oscar-nominated films.
- **LITTLE MEN:** *Little Men* is the second in the unofficial Little Women trilogy that finishes with *Jo's Boys*. It was published in 1871, and tells the story of life for students at Plumfield, a school run by Jo and her professor husband.

৩

ERNEST HEMINGWAY was born in Illinois in 1899, and died in 1961 in Idaho, where he committed suicide. He is known as one of the most important American writers of the twentieth century, and of all time. He won the Pulitzer Prize for Fiction in 1953, and the Nobel Prize for Literature in 1954.

NOTABLE ERNEST HEMINGWAY WORKS:

- ***THE SUN ALSO RISES***: Hemingway's first novel, *The Sun Also Rises*, was published in 1926. It's about a circle of American and British expatriates who travel from Paris to Spain, and is a *roman à clef* based upon Hemingway's own circle of friends. It is a portrait of the Lost Generation—young people in the 1920s forever changed by World War I.

- ***THE OLD MAN AND THE SEA***: The last major work Hemingway wrote and published in his lifetime was *The Old Man and the Sea*, which he published in 1952. It is still one of his most famous works. The story centers on Santiago, a fisherman struggling to catch a large marlin out at sea.

TONI MORRISON was born in 1931 and remains one of America's most important contemporary novelists. She is responsible for some of the most notable works of African-American literature in the twentieth century. She won the Pulitzer Prize for Fiction in 1988, the Nobel Prize for Literature in 1993, and the Presidential Medal of Freedom in 2012.

NOTABLE TONI MORRISON WORKS:

- ***THE BLUEST EYE***: Morrison's first novel, *The Bluest Eye*, first published in 1970, is about a young African-American girl named Pecola who wishes to be beautiful. The title refers to her desire to have blue eyes.

- ***BELOVED***: Published in 1987, *Beloved* is the story of Sethe and her daughter Denver who have escaped from slavery in the 1850s.

Their new home in Ohio is haunted by what Sethe believes is the ghost of a daughter she murdered to protect her from being returned to slavery, a child whose tombstone reads: Beloved. The book is often cited as one of the greatest American novels of all time.

§

With more than 350 million books sold, **STEPHEN KING** is one of the most prolific writers of the twentieth century. He was born in 1947 in Maine, where he still lives today, and has written more than fifty novels, as well as many short stories, screenplays, and works of nonfiction. He is regarded as one of the masters of the horror genre.

§

NOTABLE STEPHEN KING WORKS:

- **CARRIE:** *Carrie* was King's debut novel in 1974, and tells the story of the title character who slowly discovers she has telekinetic powers, and then uses them to take revenge on the people who have mistreated her in high school. It frequently makes the American Library Association's banned books list, and has been made into four different movies.
- **THE SHINING:** King's first hardcover bestseller, *The Shining* was published in 1977, and established King as the preeminent horror author. The novel is the story of Jack Torrance, a writer and recovering alcoholic who takes up residence at the Overlook Hotel in Colorado. Once he and his family are snowed in, supernatural forces start to affect Torrance's sanity. King followed up the book with a sequel, *Doctor Sleep*, which was released in 2013.

PERIOD 2
SCIENCE

THE UNIVERSE IS A MYSTERIOUS PLACE, and the study of science takes us from the smallest particles to the largest solar systems. Having an understanding of the key principles will help you focus your view of the world around you and how it ticks. Understanding earth science, astronomy, biology, and chemistry will show you how to think analytically and rationally, make observations, and spot patterns in your everyday life.

FRESHMAN YEAR: EARTH SCIENCE & ASTRONOMY

THE EARTH

The outermost layer of **EARTH**, the layer we are living on, is called the **CRUST**. It is the thinnest layer of Earth, and is composed of two types of rock: **GRANITE**, otherwise known as the continental crust; and **BASALT**, also known as the oceanic crust.

∽

The layer underneath the crust and above the core is known as the **MANTLE**. Mantle rock makes up around 84 percent of Earth's volume. The mantle begins around 19 miles below the continental crust and 6 miles below the oceanic crust. It can be divided into two parts: the upper and lower mantle.

∽

The **UPPER MANTLE** includes the asthenosphere, which is involved in plate tectonic movement. Part of the lithosphere, the outermost shell of the planet, is also in the upper mantle.

∽

The **LOWER MANTLE** plays a key role in controlling the planet's thermal evolution; it is located 190 to 1,800 miles below the crust, with an average temperature of 5,400°F. The lower mantle is mostly made of perovskite, a magnesium silicate mineral, which can change into a high-pressure form.

The **CORE** comprises about 15 percent of Earth's volume, is made of iron and nickel, and is roughly the size of Mars.

The **OUTER CORE** is 1,800 to 3,200 miles below Earth's surface and is made of mostly molten iron. The temperature of the molten core ranges from 7,200°F to 9,032°F. The motion of the molten core creates Earth's magnetic field.

The **INNER CORE** is 3,200 to 3,960 miles below the surface and is the hottest part of Earth, with a temperature of 9,032°F to 10,832°F. There is so much pressure in the inner core that it is actually solid metal, and is believed to be made of a nickel-iron alloy. The extreme heat of the core directly affects the movement of plate tectonics and Earth's magnetic field.

The final layer is not on the ground, but above it. The **ATMOS-PHERE** surrounds the planet and gives it life. There are several layers in the atmosphere, and it is about 500 miles thick. It is composed of various gases, dust, and water. The atmosphere provides warmth and even protection from the sun's rays and meteorites.

GEOLOGIC PERIODS

The **PALEOZOIC ERA**, the time period when life forms first began to explode in diversity, started with the **CAMBRIAN PERIOD**. The Cambrian period occurred 570 to 510 million years ago. During the Cambrian period, the supercontinent Gondwana broke apart and global temperatures began rising. Oceans were considerably higher, and though life on land was sparse, it is during this time that the first invertebrates began to appear in the oceans. While Precambrian life had soft bodies, the life found in the Cambrian period featured hard shells.

∽

The **TRIASSIC PERIOD** occurred 248 to 206 million years ago, and it was the first period of the **MESOZOIC ERA**. This period is defined by the first appearance of dinosaurs (which were no more than 15 feet tall and walked on all four legs), the first mammals (which were small and lizard-like), and flying reptiles (known as pterosaurs).

∽

The **JURASSIC PERIOD** occurred 206 to 144 million years ago, and it is considered the middle of the Mesozoic era. In the early part of the Jurassic period, Pangaea broke up into northern and southern super-continents. It is during this time that the most commonly known dinosaurs, such as stegosaurus, brachiosaurus, and allosaurus, lived. The dinosaurs that were herbivores were quite large in size, while the carnivores were smaller. Mammals were still relatively small, around the size of dogs, and the first bird, which resembled a dinosaur but had feathers, appeared.

∽

The **CRETACEOUS PERIOD** occurred 144 to 65 million years ago. It is the longest period found in the current **PHANEROZOIC EON**. While dinosaurs still thrived, and Pangaea continued to separate, it is during this time that flowering plants and new kinds of birds (which still could not fly) and mammals began to appear, as well as the first lizards and snakes. This period ended with the K-T extinction, one of the largest mass extinctions, during which all of the dinosaurs and large marine reptiles died off.

The **TERTIARY PERIOD** occurred 65 to 1.6 million years ago. This period is divided into five epochs:

- **PALEOCENE EPOCH:** The first primates appeared.
- **EOCENE EPOCH:** Aquatic mammals and modern birds started to appear.
- **OLIGOCENE EPOCH:** Featured toothed whales, cats, and dogs.
- **MIOCENE EPOCH:** Primates, horses, camels, rhinos, and beaver-like animals started to appear.
- **PLIOCENE EPOCH:** The first ancestors of modern humans, hominids, appeared and the geography of the planet was similar to what is found today.

The **QUATERNARY PERIOD**, which continues to the present, started 1.8 million years ago and began with a great **ICE AGE**. This is the age dominated by human beings and mammals. During this time, the woolly mammoth, saber-toothed tiger, and other giant mammals (known as megafauna) roamed. Today, most of the remaining megafauna are found in Africa, such as the elephant and hippopotamus. It is during the Quaternary period that the hominids evolved into modern humans, who evolved into their current form around 190,000 years ago.

NATURAL DISASTERS

Earth's crust and the mantle slowly move in separate pieces called tectonic plates. The edges of these tectonic plates are called boundaries, which are made of faults. As the plates move, the edges get stuck as the rest of the plate continues to move. When the plate finally moves far enough away, the edges of the plate get unstuck on one of the faults, and this release of energy creates an **EARTHQUAKE**.

ဟ

HURRICANES, also known as typhoons or cyclones, develop in the summer and early fall months over warm waters. The humid air travels upward, forming clouds and leaving a low-pressure area below it. Any warm air left in this area pushes into the low-pressure area and begins to rise. This process continues as the air and clouds spin. When the wind speed of this low-pressure system reaches 75 miles per hour, it is no longer a tropical storm and is officially a hurricane.

ဟ

The most common and dangerous **TORNADOES** form from a supercell thunderstorm, meaning it lasts longer than an hour and feeds off of a rising current of air that is rotating and tilted. Nonsupercell tornadoes form without the updraft of air. A gustnado is a form of a nonsupercell tornado that forms near the ground from dust or debris, and a landspout is a nonsupercell tornado that forms near the ground, doesn't have a rotating updraft, and forms a funnel when the thunderstorm cloud is growing. Waterspouts are like landspouts, but they form over water.

ဟ

AVALANCHES occur because of gravity's pull on the snow on a mountainside. In mild weather, water vapor can slide down the snow, flake, and refreeze at the center, creating a cohesive and solid mass. When it is cold, the water vapor goes to the bottom of the snow on the ground and forms angular crystals, which weaken snow. Sunlight and light rain produce a thin surface crust, and that makes bonding of new snow more difficult. Instability of the snowpack can be triggered by a storm, wind, temperature, and even a person's weight.

Sluffs are avalanches of loose snow, and slab avalanches occur when a strong layer is on top of a weak layer, and are the deadlier type.

∽

TSUNAMIS are caused by shifts in the seafloor, and are generally the result of earthquakes, landslides, or volcanic eruptions. For a tsunami to occur, the earthquake must occur near or under the ocean, with vertical movements in the seafloor. Large amounts of energy are dispersed in an upward bottom movement, and a wave forms.

∽

VOLCANOES are mountains that were formed from folded continental plates. The magma that erupts from the volcano comes from 150 kilometers below Earth's crust, where there is enormous pressure. This pressure forces the magma to rise, creating the eruption. When magma is released, it is then referred to as lava.

THE SOLAR SYSTEM

THE SOLAR SYSTEM consists of the Sun, Earth, Mars, Mercury, Venus, Jupiter, Saturn, Neptune, Uranus, moons orbiting the planets, dwarf planets, and the asteroid belt.

∽

The solar system has an elliptical shape and is always in motion. The solar system is believed to be about 4 billion years old.

∽

There are eight planets in the solar system. **MERCURY, VENUS, EARTH,** and **MARS** are known as rocky inner planets. These are smaller and denser, contain less gas, and are primarily composed of rock or metals. In fact, Mercury and Mars do not even have atmospheres.

The other four planets, **JUPITER, SATURN, NEPTUNE,** and **URA-NUS**, known as outer planets, are larger, with dense atmospheres and small cores.

∽

The **SUN** is the center of the solar system, the closest star, and the largest object in the solar system. It makes up 99.8 percent of the mass of the solar system. The power of the Sun is produced through nuclear fusion reactions. The energy from the nuclear fusion travels into space in the form of light and heat. The surface of the Sun has a temperature of 5,800 kelvin.

∽

ASTEROIDS are bits of rock that were left over after the formation of the Sun and the planets. These asteroids are most often found orbiting the Sun between Mars and Jupiter. This area is known as the **ASTEROID BELT**, and more than 7,000 asteroids have been discovered in it. The total mass of the asteroids found in the asteroid belt is less than the mass of the Moon.

∽

The **MILKY WAY** is the spiral-shaped galaxy that is the home to our solar system. Whereas the solar system revolves around one sun, the Milky Way contains at least 400 billion other stars (with their planets and other objects in orbit). The Milky Way is just one of 200 billion galaxies that have been observed from Earth.

∽

Until fairly recently, **PLUTO** was referred to as another planet in our solar system; however, it is now referred to as a **DWARF PLANET**. Dwarf planets orbit around the Sun, have a mass that gravity has turned round, cannot be satellites to other planets, and have a mass that is larger than an asteroid but not large enough to be considered a planet. Dwarf planets are not categories of planets, but rather different objects entirely. There are three dwarf planets in our solar system: Pluto, Ceres, and Eris.

EXTRACURRICULARS: DRAMA CLUB

In 2011, **NASA** compiled a list of the least plausible science fiction movies of all time: *2012* (2009), *The Core* (2003), and *Armageddon* (1998) topped the list. The most realistic were *Gattaca* (1997), *Contact* (1997), and *Metropolis* (1927).

SOPHOMORE YEAR: BIOLOGY

THE CELL

The **CELL** is the smallest unit of life in an organism's body. Each cell has its own unique feature and function.

∽

Some organisms, like humans, animals, and plants, are **MULTICELLULAR**, meaning they are made of many, many cells (for humans the number is in the trillions). However, other organisms, such as bacteria, are **UNICELLULAR**, meaning they consist of a single cell.

∽

There are two basic types of cells: prokaryotic and eukaryotic. **PROKARYOTIC** means "before a nucleus," and **EUKARYOTIC** means "possessing a true nucleus." Prokaryotic cells have no nucleus, are usually single-celled organisms, and were the first organisms to live on Earth. Examples of prokaryotic cells are bacteria. On the other hand, eukaryotic cells have a nucleus and organelles, and are the types of cells found in humans, plants, and animals.

∽

PLANT CELLS have very rigid walls made of cellulose and contain chloroplasts. Chloroplasts, which contain chlorophyll, utilize the Sun's light and enable the process of photosynthesis. They are also responsible for the green color found in plants. Plant cells have a larger central vacuole and contain, within their cell walls, linking pores that connect to transmit information.

∽

ANIMAL CELLS are much smaller than plant cells and do not have the rigid cell walls that plant cells have. This allows animal cells to take on various shapes. While plants have the ability to make their own food with chloroplasts and sunlight, in animal cells, it is the role of the mitochondria to get energy from food that is consumed.

∽

The **PLASMA MEMBRANE** is the outer lining of a eukaryote cell. It protects the cell from the surrounding environment and is composed of lipids and proteins. The nucleus inside of a cell is surrounded by a membrane that separates it from the cytoplasm.

∽

Two kinds of genetic material, **DNA** and **RNA**, exist inside the cell. The cell's chromosomes are in the nucleus, which is also the location for RNA synthesis and DNA replication.

∽

The **NUCLEUS** is responsible for regulating all activity in eukaryotic cells. It contains the hereditary information (DNA and RNA) and controls growth and reproduction. The most prominent structure in the nucleus is called the nucleolus.

∽

The **NUCLEOLUS** produces ribosomes, which play a critical role in protein synthesis. These proteins are used for a variety of purposes including, but not limited to, structural support and as enzymes to catalyze a reaction.

MITOSIS

Plants and even some animals reproduce in a different way—asexually, or without a mate. This is done through mitosis. **MITOSIS** is a process of cell division that involves replicating chromosome material. During asexual reproduction, genetic mixing does not happen, and it is sometimes referred to as cloning because the copies are identical.

∽

During **INTERPHASE**, the cell prepares for mitosis. The next step in the cycle is **PROPHASE**, when the chromatin will condense and become chromosomes, which have duplicated and now have sister chromatids. The chromatids are identical to each other and are connected, forming an X. The mitotic spindle, which moves the chromosomes, is formed and set up away from the nucleus. By the end of this step the nuclear envelope is broken down into vesicles.

∽

In **METAPHASE**, chromosomes are aligned along the middle of the nucleus of the cell and are held in place by microtubules of spindle fibers. This is known as the metaphase plate. Chromosomes are oriented so that kinetochores, a protein structure on the chromosomes, are facing the pole, and each tail of the chromosomes is facing each other. The organization allows for the new nuclei to receive a single copy of each chromosome when separation occurs in the next phase.

ഗ

During the **ANAPHASE**, the chromosomes that are paired begin to separate at the kinetochores. The kinetochores then start to move toward the poles. Once this has happened, the polar fibers will elongate, which start to spread the poles farther apart from each other. The sister chromatids then separate and move toward their related poles.

ഗ

In the **TELOPHASE**, once the chromatids have reached their opposite poles, new membranes begin to form around the sets of chromosomes, forming two nuclei. These two nuclei are, for the time being, in the same cell. RNA synthesis occurs and the nuclear envelope reappears, which then breaks down the chromosomes to the point where they can no longer be viewed with a light microscope.

ഗ

After telophase, there are two nuclei in a single cell. All that is left is for the cell to divide in half. **CYTOKINESIS** actually begins during anaphase and continues simultaneously through telophase. The cell first begins to furrow, a process where it starts pinching in. The cell pinches until there are two daughter cells, each with its own nucleus. These two cells will then continue the cycle.

ഗ

MEIOSIS is a cell division that occurs to produce germ cells like the sperm and egg, and thus is a necessity for sexual reproduction. In meiosis, a copy of the mother's chromosomes and a copy of the father's chromosomes is replicated. Four haploid cells are produced, each with one copy of a chromosome. This process is responsible for creating genetic diversity, because each cell has its own unique combination of chromosomes. A single parent cell will create four daughter cells, and each daughter cell has half the amount of chromosomes as the parent cell.

PHOTOSYNTHESIS

PHOTOSYNTHESIS is the process that plants and some bacteria perform to convert the energy that comes from sunlight into usable energy. The sunlight is first turned into a sugar, and then through a process called **CELLULAR RESPIRATION**, the sugar is turned into adenosine triphosphate, known as **ATP**, a form of energy. Plants require water and carbon dioxide, and as a result of photosynthesis, oxygen is released into the atmosphere. Without photosynthesis, life would not exist.

∽

Leaves play a critical role in allowing carbon dioxide and water in and allowing oxygen and sugar to escape during photosynthesis. As water comes in through the roots of the plant, it is transported to the leaves via cells. A waxy layer, called the cuticle, covers the leaf. This waxy layer prevents carbon dioxide from entering and oxygen from escaping. As a result, leaves have tiny openings called stomata (*stoma* is the singular term), which allow the carbon dioxide to pass out and the oxygen to enter.

∽

The **LIGHT-DEPENDENT PROCESS** (also known as light reactions) that occurs in the chloroplasts and thylakoids; it is a stage in which light energy is absorbed by the chlorophyll and converted into chemical energy. During this process, water is split and oxygen is released. Light reactions have two photosystems (photosystem I and photosystem II), which harvest the light. The chlorophyll in photosystem I is the stronger absorber of light. The two products produced by light reactions are ATP and NADPH$_2$.

§

The **LIGHT-INDEPENDENT PROCESS** (or dark reaction) occurs in the stromata of chloroplasts, and removes carbon dioxide from the atmosphere and turns it into glucose with the ATP and NADPH$_2$ from the light-dependent process. For this process to occur light is not necessary, and no matter how much light is available, the process can continue. A 5-carbon sugar is combined with carbon dioxide, creating a 6-carbon sugar. This sugar is then broken into fructose and glucose, which sucrose is made of.

§

As animals produce carbon dioxide from breathing, plants take in the carbon dioxide and use it to make organic nutrients. The plant is then eaten by an animal (transferring the carbon), and then that animal is eaten by another animal (once again transferring the carbon). When plants and animals die and decompose, carbon enters the ground. Some of that carbon is buried and eventually turns into fossil fuel. As humans use fossil fuels, carbon is released into the atmosphere in the form of carbon dioxide gas. The carbon then travels from the atmosphere into the oceans and other bodies of water. This process is known as the **CARBON CYCLE**.

GENETICS

Austrian monk **GREGOR MENDEL** is considered to be the father of **GENETICS**. In 1856, Mendel conducted a series of studies on pea plants observing seven traits he found in the plants: the color and shape of the seed, the color of the flower, the color and shape of the pod, the position of the flower, and the height of the plant. Mendel performed tests in hybridization and cross-pollination and found that the first generation of plants only resembled one parent, but in the next generations, dominant and recessive traits appeared.

∽

Mendel came up with three laws regarding inheritance:

1. **THE LAW OF DOMINANCE:** if there is a pair of genes, the one that appears in the offspring is most likely the dominant one because that is passed on more often than the recessive gene.
2. **THE PRINCIPLE OF SEGREGATION:** an individual inherits an allele (or a unit of information) about a trait from both parents, and during the formation of the gamete, these alleles segregate from one another.
3. **THE LAW OF INDEPENDENT ASSORTMENT:** the factors for characteristics are distributed independently to the reproductive cells.

∽

In **SINGLE-GENE INHERITANCE**, also known as Mendelian inheritance, a single gene is mutated and then follows the predictable pattern of inheritance.

∽

In **MULTIFACTORIAL INHERITANCE**, it is not due to a single gene but rather several genes and environmental factors.

∽

In **MITOCHONDRIAL INHERITANCE**, disease is transmitted by the mitochondria, organelles that are inherited only from the mother's egg.

∽

Deoxyribonucleic acid, or **DNA**, is a double-helix structure that carries all the genetic information and is the hereditary material. The double-helix structure is crucial in genetics. DNA can copy and replicate itself, and each strand in the double helix serves as a pattern for duplication. When cells divide, each new cell gets an exact copy of the old cell's DNA.

တ

GENE EXPRESSION is the process of converting the gene's information into **MESSENGER RNA** (mRNA) through a process called transcription, and then converting the information to a protein in a process called translation. Gene expression is responsible for interpreting the genetic code in the DNA, which gives rise to the organism's traits, or phenotype.

> **EXTRACURRICULARS: YEARBOOK**
> **MOST LIKELY TO BE MISTAKEN FOR**
> **SOMEONE ELSE**
> In 1996, **DOLLY** the sheep became the first mammal to be cloned. She was born in Scotland, and her DNA was taken from another adult cell. Since then, other mammals have been successfully cloned, but none will ever be as famous as Dolly, who died at the age of six in 2003.

JUNIOR YEAR: CHEMISTRY

THE PERIODIC TABLE

The **PERIODIC TABLE** is a table displaying the various atomic elements. There are currently 118 known elements. The elements are placed along the grid in accordance with how they look and how they act. Rows and columns also have particular meaning in the periodic table. If elements are in the same row (each row is considered a period), that means they have something in common. The elements in the center of the table are known as transition elements.

∽

The periodic table used today was created by Dmitri Mendeleev in 1869; however, he was not the first. In 1789, a list of thirty-three chemical elements was published, organized by earths, gases, metals, and nonmetals. In 1829, Johann Wolfgang Döbereiner came to the realization that based on chemical properties, elements could be organized into groups of three, or triads. By 1869, there had been several attempts at perfecting the table, and what made Mendeleev's table so special was that it left gaps for elements not yet discovered. Also, it occasionally ignored the order by atomic weight to better classify into chemical families.

∽

The vertical columns in the periodic table are called **GROUPS**. The groups are the most important way to classify elements. In the current format, the groups are numbered 1 to 18 from the left to the right. Elements in a group share similar configurations of the atom's outermost electron shells. The groups are given names such as alkali metals, alkaline earth metals, halogens, pnictogens, and chalcogens, to name a few.

∽

The horizontal rows in the periodic table are known as **PERIODS**. All the elements in a period have the same number of electron shells. Currently, the maximum number of electron shells for any type of element is seven. As you move across a period, the atomic number increases. The atomic number is the number of protons found in the atom's nucleus.

∽

A set of adjacent groups is known as a **BLOCK** or **FAMILY**. There are five blocks: s-block (the first two groups), p-block (the last six groups except for helium), d-block (the transition metals), f-block (part of the lanthanoids and actinoids), and g-block (which is hypothetical; no elements exist in the g-block yet). These blocks reflect the configuration of the electrons.

∽

The naming of the elements is complex. Sometimes it is just the first letter of the element (such as oxygen, O; or hydrogen, H), sometimes it's the beginning of the Latin word (gold is Au, from the Latin *aurum*), while other times it is named for the person who discovered it or for a whole slew of other reasons (polonium is Po, which stands for Poland, named after the country that the people who discovered the element were from).

∽

A **CHEMICAL FORMULA** is a method of expressing how a chemical appears in a simple and easy to understand way based on the atoms that make up chemical compounds. When writing out the elements involved in a chemical, if there is more than one atom present in a particular element, then it is indicated by a subscript number after the symbol, showing how many atoms there are. For example, water is H_2O. This means there are two hydrogen atoms and one oxygen atom present in water.

∽

IONS are atoms that have a positive or negative charge. This is due to the fact that the number of electrons in the atom is not the same as the number of protons. Ions can be represented with a superscript on the right-hand side showing whether it is positive or negative. For example, Na^+. In more complex ions, brackets are used (and parentheses can be used inside the brackets).

✍

POLYMERS are macromolecules made up of structural units that repeat. When writing the formula of a polymer, you do not have to write out every one of the repeating units. Instead, parentheses are used followed by a subscript to show how many times it repeats. For example, in a hydrocarbon molecule described as $CH_3(CH_2)_{50}CH_3$ the CH_2 repeats fifty times.

✍

ISOTOPES are different versions of the same element having different numbers of neutrons. Isotopes are indicated with a superscript number on the left-hand side of the formula. For example, the isotope Uranium 235 is expressed as ^{235}U. The 235 refers to the number of neutrons and protons combined, or the mass number.

✍

The **EMPIRICAL FORMULA** is the simplest way of expressing the ratio of the elements present in a compound. For example, the molecular formula for glucose is $C_6H_{12}O_6$. However, the empirical formula breaks that down further into its simplest form. So glucose expressed in the empirical formula is CH_2O.

Another system of writing chemical formulas is called the **HILL SYS-TEM**. With the Hill system, you first indicate the number of carbon atoms, then hydrogen, and then you go down the list of elements alphabetically. For example, uranium oxide in the chemical formula is written as U_3O_8. In the Hill system, it appears as O_8U_3. This system is commonly used for databases.

SOLIDS, LIQUIDS, AND GASES

SOLIDS are made up of atoms, molecules, or ions in a fixed and rigid position with very little space between them.

Particles in solids cannot be easily compressed or move and slide past each other. They are usually arranged in a regular pattern.

When atoms, molecules, or ions are not arranged in a regular pattern, move past each other easily, and assume the shape of their container, they are known as **LIQUID**.

Liquids are not easily compressed, but flow easily.

GASES are very easily compressible. The atoms, molecules, or ions in a gas vibrate and move at high speeds.

SOME GAS LAWS:

- **BOYLE'S LAW:** States that if temperature is constant, there is an inversely proportional relationship between volume and absolute pressure. The equation for Boyle's law is represented as:

$$pV = k$$

p is the pressure, V is the volume, and k is a constant, which is found by multiplying the pressure by the volume. Because there is an inverse relationship between volume and pressure, if the volume is doubled, the pressure would be inverted, which means that one-half of the pressure is being used.

- **CHARLES'S LAW:** In the late 1700s, Jacques Charles and Joseph Louis Gay-Lussac studied how gas volume was affected by the gas's temperature. Charles's law, which is also called the law of volumes, shows that when heated, gas expands. Charles's law can be depicted as:

$$V \propto T$$

V represents volume and T represents absolute temperature. In each formula, the volume of gas increases proportionally when the absolute temperature increases.

- **GAY-LUSSAC'S LAW:** Builds upon Boyle's law and Charles's law, and actually represents two ideas. The first part is known as the law of combining volumes. This law states that gases combine in simple proportions (for example, water is simply two parts hydrogen and one part oxygen). The other part of Gay-Lussac's law is the pressure-temperature law. This law states that pressure of an amount of gas at a constant volume is proportional to the absolute temperature.

- **AVOGADRO'S LAW:** In 1811, Italian chemist Amedeo Avogadro hypothesized that two gases with the same pressure, volume, and temperature would also contain the same number of molecules, regardless of any physical or chemical properties. Avogadro's law can be written as:

$$\frac{V}{n} = k$$

V represents the volume, n represents the number of moles (or substance) in the gas, and k is a constant.

From Avogadro's law, it was determined that the ideal gas constant (k) is the same value for any gas, which means:

$$\frac{p_1 \bullet V_1}{T_1 \bullet n_1} = \frac{p_2 \bullet V_2}{T_2 \bullet n_2} = \text{constant}$$

- **GRAHAM'S LAW:** Graham's law deals with effusion, the process where molecules escape from a container through a hole and do not collide. Graham's law states that the rate of effusion is inversely proportional to the square root of the molecular masses. Graham's law can be written as:

$$\frac{\text{Rate}_1}{\text{Rate}_2} = \frac{\sqrt{M_2}}{\sqrt{M_1}}$$

Rate_1 and Rate_2 are the rates of effusion for the first and second gases, respectively, and M_1 and M_2 are the molar masses of the first and second gases, respectively.

Though the three best-known phases of matter are solid, liquid, and gas, there is a fourth phase known as **PLASMA**. It is the most abundant form of matter in the entire universe even though it does not have a definite form. Plasma is matter that has a very high pressure and temperature, and stars and interstellar dust feature plasma (for example, it is found on the Sun). Plasma is a combination of free electrons (which are stripped from their orbit), neutral atoms, and charged ions. Like gas and liquid, plasma is fluid; however, due to the charged particles, it both responds to electro-magnetic forces and generates electromagnetic forces.

NEWTON'S LAWS OF MOTION

NEWTON'S FIRST LAW OF MOTION: Objects at rest stay at rest, and objects in motion stay in a straight line at a constant speed unless an unbalanced force acts on it. If the sum of all of the forces, or net force, is zero, there will be no acceleration or change in velocity. If the net force does not equal zero, there will be acceleration and a change in velocity.

NEWTON'S SECOND LAW OF MOTION: If one puts force on an object, its acceleration, or velocity, will change in the direction you force it to. The acceleration is directly proportional to force (if you push twice as hard on something, it goes twice as fast). The acceleration is inversely proportional to the mass. His second law can be summarized as $F = ma$, where F is force, m is mass, and a is acceleration.

NEWTON'S THIRD LAW OF MOTION: With every force, there is an opposite and equal force. In other words, for every *F*, there is a –*F*. If you push on something, it will push back. When two objects collide, an opposite and equal force is present.

SENIOR YEAR: HUMAN ANATOMY AND PHYSIOLOGY

THE NERVOUS SYSTEM

The **NERVOUS SYSTEM** is a complex system that is responsible for sending every electrical impulse and signal throughout your body. These signals are what cause any and all actions, reactions, and thoughts you have, as well as anything you feel. The nervous system is made up of two systems: the central nervous system and the peripheral nervous system.

ιᴨ

The nervous system works via nerve cells, or **NEURONS**. These cells process and transmit information through chemical and electrical signaling. What makes neurons different from other cells is that they have very specialized extensions called axons and dendrites. Dendrites receive the information, and the axon carries the message to target cells.

The **CENTRAL NERVOUS SYSTEM** consists of two of the most important parts of the nervous system: the brain and the spinal cord. The brain is considered to be the command center of the nervous system, since it controls all of the workings of your body. The central nervous system collaborates with the peripheral nervous system in controlling the behavior of the body.

The **PERIPHERAL NERVOUS SYSTEM** consists of the nerves that receive and send the information from the central nervous system. There are two types of nerves: motor nerves, which send signals from the brain to different tissues in the body; and sensory nerves, which receive information in the form of pain, heat, or touch and then send those impulses to the central nervous system.

The **SOMATIC NERVOUS SYSTEM**, or voluntary nervous system, is part of the peripheral nervous system. It is responsible for processing sensory information—such as pain, heat, and touch—from an external stimuli, and controlling the voluntary muscular systems. The somatic nervous system allows a person to receive sensory information and react to environmental changes. The somatic nervous system is also part of the autonomic nervous system.

The **AUTONOMIC NERVOUS SYSTEM** is part of the peripheral nervous system and controls involuntary body functions. Two important aspects of the autonomic nervous system are the sympathetic nervous system, which comes into effect causing the fight-or-flight reaction; and the parasympathetic nervous system, which comes into effect in nonemergency situations, causing the body to rest and relax.

THE CIRCULATORY SYSTEM

The **CIRCULATORY SYSTEM** consists of the heart, blood, and blood vessels. It is the body's transportation and cooling system. Your blood is pumped from the heart via arteries, and to your heart via veins, delivering oxygen and nutrients throughout your body. The blood also picks up any waste products in your system so the body can get rid of them.

ᴄᴏ

The **HEART** is a muscle roughly the size of a clenched fist. It is two sided and has four chambers. Blood enters the heart through the right atrium. The **RIGHT VENTRICLE** pushes the deoxygenated blood to the lungs. The **LEFT ATRIUM** then receives the oxygenated blood and pumps it to the **LEFT VENTRICLE** of the heart, which is responsible for pushing the blood out of the heart and into the body's circulation.

ᴄᴏ

BLOOD is constantly flowing through our bodies and carries oxygen, nutrients, water, and waste products to and from our cells. **RED BLOOD CELLS** carry oxygen and carbon dioxide. After picking up oxygen from the lungs and delivering it to the cells, the red blood cells transport the carbon dioxide to the lungs, from which it is then exhaled.

ᴄᴏ

WHITE BLOOD CELLS fight germs. During an infection, the body produces more white blood cells, which will then try to attack and destroy the infection. When someone is prescribed an antibiotic, it is because the white blood cells need help fighting off the infection.

ᴄᴏ

The **AORTA** is the largest artery in the body. It originates from the left ventricle and distributes the oxygenated blood. From the aorta, the blood is then sent to the other arteries and arterioles, which are small arteries that deliver oxygen and nutrients to all of the cells in your body. At the end of the arterioles are capillaries, which pass the blood through the venous system.

ᴜᴏ

The **VENOUS SYSTEM** is responsible for bringing the blood back to the heart. From the capillaries, the blood flows through small veins called venules, and from there, the blood then flows to the veins. The superior and inferior venae cavae are the two largest veins in the body, and both end in the right atrium. The superior vena cava enters on the top while the inferior enters from the bottom.

THE RESPIRATORY SYSTEM

The function of the **RESPIRATORY SYSTEM** is to supply the blood with oxygen, which is then transferred to the rest of the body. Oxygen is received through breathing. The oxygen enters through the nose and mouth. From there, it goes through the larynx and trachea to the chest cavity, where the trachea then splits into small tubes called bronchi. The bronchus then divides once more, creating bronchial tubes, which lead to the **LUNGS**.

ᴜᴏ

Inside the lungs are tiny sacs called **ALVEOLI**. The inhaled oxygen passes through the alveoli and then diffuses into the arterial blood through the capillaries. As this is happening, the veins send waste-laden blood carrying carbon dioxide into the alveoli and this carbon dioxide comes out as you exhale. Both inhalation and exhalation are made possible by the diaphragm muscle below the lungs, which contracts and relaxes.

The nose and throat are the first line of defense when it comes to protecting the respiratory system. As air is inhaled through the nose, the dirt is cleaned by the hairs in the nose, and further cleaned by mucus. The nasal cavity is lined with tissue that consists of many blood vessels. These blood vessels provide heat, which warms the air as it is taken in. The nasal cavity also adds moisture to this air, making it suitable for the lungs.

THE DIGESTIVE SYSTEM

When a person eats, the saliva in the mouth has **ENZYMES** that start to break down the chemicals in the food. As your teeth chew the food, you begin to further break it down into a mushy substance. The tongue then rolls this substance into a ball, and the food is now called bolus, meaning a substance that is broken down to the point that is ready to be swallowed.

The tongue pushes the food to the back of the throat, toward the opening of the esophagus. The **ESOPHAGUS** is a pipe responsible for moving food from the throat to the stomach. When a person swallows, a little flap called the epiglottis closes the windpipe, ensuring the food goes down the esophagus. Along the walls of the esophagus, muscles squeeze the food, until it reaches the stomach.

The **STOMACH** has three roles: to store food, to break down the food into chyme (a semifluid paste), and to empty the chyme into the small intestine. The stomach breaks down the food with the help of gastric juices that line the walls of the organ. The gastric juices start breaking down the food to its essential nutrients, and kill any harmful bacteria that may be in the food.

∽

From the stomach, the food enters the **SMALL INTESTINE**, an organ that, outstretched, is 22 feet long in an adult. The small intestine breaks down the food further and it is where the major amount of absorption of nutrients takes place. The nutrients are then sent to the liver, while what's left of the food is passed on to the large intestine.

∽

The **LARGE INTESTINE** measures 5 feet long and is fatter than the small intestine. What the small intestine passes on to the large intestine is waste. There is no longer any nutritional value to the substance, so therefore the body can't use it and it must be expelled. The substance passes through a part of the large intestine called the colon, which is the last chance to absorb any water or minerals. The result is feces, and the large intestine then pushes this solid waste to the rectum.

∽

The liver, gallbladder, and pancreas also play a key role in the digestive system. These organs send digestive juices to the small intestine. The **PANCREAS** is responsible for sending juices that digest protein and fat. **BILE**, a substance created by the liver but stored in the **GALLBLADDER**, absorbs fat in the bloodstream. The nutrient-rich blood is then sent to the **LIVER**, where waste is filtered out.

THE REPRODUCTIVE SYSTEM

The **REPRODUCTION SYSTEM** is a system of organs that work together and allow humans to reproduce. In order for reproduction to occur, two different types of reproduction systems must be present: the male reproduction system and the female reproduction system. The differences between these systems allow for the genetic material of both individuals to be passed on to the offspring.

∽

There are two types of **GAMETES**, or sex cells, involved in human reproduction. The male gamete is called the **SPERM** and the female gamete is called the **OVUM**, or egg. The gametes are produced in organs called gonads. In the male, the sperm is produced in the testes, and in the female, the ovum is produced in the ovaries. Each gamete carries twenty-three chromosomes. The ovum carries only an X chromosome, and the sperm can carry either an X or a Y chromosome. During sexual intercourse, the gametes come together in fertilization. If both have an X chromosome, the zygote will grow to become a female. If the sperm has a Y chromosome, it will become a male.

∽

The role of the **MALE REPRODUCTIVE SYSTEM** is to produce semen, which transports the sperm during sexual intercourse. The external structures of the male reproduction system include the penis, the organ used during sexual intercourse; the scrotum, a sac that holds and moderates the temperature of the testicles; and the testicles, which make testosterone and generate sperm. There are several internal structures involved in the male reproduction system including the epididymis, a tube that transports, stores, and matures the sperm; and the vas deferens, a tube that transports the mature sperm to the urethra, which passes urine and semen out of the body.

∽

The **FEMALE REPRODUCTIVE SYSTEM** is responsible for producing the egg cells and hormones and transporting the egg cells to the site of fertilization; if conception occurs, the beginning stages of pregnancy take place. If fertilization does not happen, the system is designed to shed the uterine lining, or menstruate. The female reproductive system is located internally in the pelvis and consists of the vagina, the cervix, the uterus (the major organ that accommodates the growing fetus and pushes the fetus out during delivery), the fallopian tubes (the source of fertilization), and the ovaries.

ⓢ

Immediately upon fertilization, the sex of the child is determined. In the first four weeks, neural tubes, the foundation of the nervous system, develop and the heart and a primitive circulatory system form. By the third week, the embryo has developed along with a placenta, and its heart begins to beat. By day 40, the embryo is the size of a raspberry and has five fingers on each hand, and its brain waves can be detected. By week 12, the fetus breathes amniotic fluid, sleeps, awakens, and can open and close its mouth. By week 21, the fetus now weighs 1 pound. By week 36, the baby will weigh anywhere from 6 to 9 pounds. By week 38, its heartbeat can be heard from outside the womb and the baby is ready to come out.

BODY TISSUE

In the body, specific cells group together to perform a certain specialized function, creating tissue. When many tissues group together to carry out a specific function, it becomes an organ.

ⓢ

EPITHELIAL TISSUE is tissue that covers the entire body, and it forms the covering or lining of internal and external surfaces. It is made up of closely packed cells formed into one or many layers, with close to no intercellular spaces and little intercellular substance.

Endothelium is the tissue on the surface of the internal cavities, and its main function is for absorption, excretion, protection, secretion, reproduction, and sensory reception.

∽

CONNECTIVE TISSUE supports and binds to other tissues in the body. It is the framework that epithelial tissue rests upon, and it is what nerve and muscle tissues are embedded in. The major cells involved in immunological defense are also found in the connective tissue, and connective tissue is where inflammation, the body's defense against invading microorganisms, occurs.

∽

MUSCLE TISSUE can contract and conduct electrical impulses and allow the body to move. Muscle is classified as voluntary or involuntary, and smooth or striated. There are three types of muscle tissue: skeletal muscle (which is voluntary, striated, and attached to the bone); cardiac muscle (which is involuntary, striated, and found in the heart); and smooth muscle (which is involuntary, smooth, and found in the digestive system, respiratory system, eyes, and the walls of blood vessels).

∽

NERVOUS TISSUE is made up of neurons (cells that transmit messages) and neuroglia cells (cells that protect the neurons). Nervous tissue is specialized to conduct impulses and react to various stimuli, and it is the main part of the nervous system. Nervous tissue consists of the brain, the spinal cord (making up the central nervous system), and the peripheral nerves (making the peripheral nervous system).

∽

ORGANS are groups of tissues that work together to perform a specific function. In organs, there is usually a main tissue called the parenchyma, which is unique to the specific organ, and sporadic tissue called stroma, such as connective tissue or blood. Groups of organs that work together to perform a specific function form organ systems.

BONES

A typical human **SKELETON** is made up of about 206 bones.

ᔕ

The **VERTEBRAL COLUMN** consists of seven cervical vertebrae, twelve thoracic vertebrae, five lumbar vertebrae, the sacral vertebrae, and the coccygeal vertebrae.

ᔕ

The **CHEST** is made up of the thorax, sternum, and twelve pairs of ribs.

ᔕ

The **SKULL** is made of eight cranial bones, fifteen facial bones, and six inner-ear bones.

EXTRACURRICULARS: NEWSPAPER
SCOPES FOUND GUILTY OF TEACHING EVOLUTION

In 1925, **JOHN THOMAS SCOPES**, a substitute high-school teacher in Dayton, Tennessee, was accused of violating the state's Butler Act, which made teaching evolution illegal in a state-funded school. Scopes was found guilty and was fined $100, though the verdict was later overturned. The trial was largely seen as a stunt to bring publicity to the debate between evolution and creationism. It was later dramatized in the play *Inherit the Wind*.

Your **ARM** bones are called the clavicle, scapula, humerus, ulna, and radius, and there are twenty-seven bones in each of your hands.

Your **LEG** bones are the pelvis, femur, patella (knee cap), tibia, and fibula, and there are twenty-six bones in each of your feet.

PERIOD 3
GEOGRAPHY

IN THE AGE OF GOOGLE EARTH AND GPS, it may not seem like geography is an important skill anymore, but that's just not true. Geography is so much more than just knowing how to get from Point A to Point B. People who study geography think about Earth, the things that are found on its surface, and the people, animals, and plants that live on it. Geography is the study of oceans, earthquakes, and mountains. It is the study of populations, food supplies, and climate. It is also the study of kangaroos, whales, and deserts. This class will give you an overview of how to look at the world like a geographer.

FRESHMAN YEAR: U.S. GEOGRAPHY

THE UNITED STATES

Some basic facts about the **UNITED STATES:**

- **CAPITAL:** Washington, DC
- **AREA:** 3.54 million square miles
- **POPULATION:** 318 million
- **NATIONAL HOLIDAY:** Independence Day (July 4)

ഗ

The first people to live in **NEW ENGLAND** were the Algonquin-speaking Native Americans, including the Abenaki, the Penobscot, and the Wampanoag. The early European settlers in this area were English Protestants who wanted to be able to practice their religion freely without being punished by the Church of England. New England is famous for its authors, poets, and philosophers. The nation's first college, Harvard University, is in Cambridge, Massachusetts. It was founded in 1636.

NEW ENGLAND		
State	**Capital**	**Nickname**
Connecticut	Hartford	Constitution State
Maine	Augusta	Pine Tree State
Massachusetts	Boston	Bay State
New Hampshire	Concord	Granite State
Rhode Island	Providence	Ocean State
Vermont	Montpelier	Green Mountain State

ʊᴧ

Settled by a wider variety of Europeans than New England or the South, the **MID-ATLANTIC STATES** continue to attract people of many backgrounds. From casinos and amusement parks to clambakes and Pennsylvania Dutch, the Mid-Atlantic region is a very interesting place.

ʊᴧ

WASHINGTON, DC, is in the Mid-Atlantic area, but it is not a state so it doesn't have its own capital city or a nickname. But it is the capital of the United States, and it is home to the White House, the Washington Monument, the Smithsonian Institution, and other tourist attractions.

THE MID-ATLANTIC		
State	Capital	Nickname
Delaware	Dover	First State
Maryland	Annapolis	Old Line State
New Jersey	Trenton	Garden State
New York	Albany	Empire State
Pennsylvania	Harrisburg	Keystone State

ʊᴧ

Heading west through Pennsylvania, we enter Ohio and the **MID-WEST**, sometimes referred to as the Heartland because it's located in the center, or the heart, of the country. Big cities like Chicago, Minneapolis, and Saint Paul are major business centers, while farms in Wisconsin and Iowa grow crops that are exported around the country. However, when the farming isn't as successful, places like Iowa change their industries to computer manufacturing or insurance.

Waterways are very important to the economy in the Midwest. The Mississippi and Missouri Rivers—the two longest rivers in the United States—are major routes for shipping and travel throughout the area. Minnesota's twin cities, Minneapolis and Saint Paul, lie on either side of the Mississippi. The Mississippi and Missouri rivers actually meet each other near Saint Louis, Missouri. And there are transportation routes within the five **GREAT LAKES** (Michigan, Superior, Erie, Ontario, and Huron) as well.

THE MIDWEST		
State	**Capital**	**Nickname**
Illinois	Springfield	Prairie State
Indiana	Indianapolis	Hoosier State
Iowa	Des Moines	Hawkeye State
Missouri	Jefferson City	Show Me State
Michigan	Lansing	Wolverine State
Minnesota	Saint Paul	Gopher State
Ohio	Columbus	Buckeye State
Wisconsin	Madison	Badger State

There are several rivers that cut through the **PLAINS** states—the Missouri, the Arkansas, and the Kansas. There are the North and South Dakota Badlands, and in central Nebraska there are the Sand Hills—sand dunes held together by the grass growing on them. Climb up into the Black Hills of South Dakota and you'll see four presidents' faces staring down at you from **MOUNT RUSHMORE**. Each face is 60 feet high. The sculptor, Gutzon Borglum, carved the faces into the hills from 1927 to 1941.

THE PLAINS		
State	Capital	Nickname
Kansas	Topeka	Sunflower State
Nebraska	Lincoln	Cornhusker State
North Dakota	Bismarck	Flickertail State
South Dakota	Pierre	Mount Rushmore State

Today, the **SOUTH** has lots of industries. The warm climate is ideal for growing oranges in Florida, rice in Louisiana and Arkansas, peaches in Georgia, and many other crops. West Virginia's main industry is mining, and North Carolina is the furniture capital of the United States. Along the Gulf Coast, fishermen catch shrimp and oysters to sell. The headquarters for Coca-Cola are in Atlanta, Georgia. Tourists flock to the South for food, history, and fun.

THE SOUTH		
State	Capital	Nickname
Alabama	Montgomery	Heart of Dixie
Arkansas	Little Rock	Land of Opportunity
Florida	Tallahassee	Sunshine State
Georgia	Atlanta	Empire State of the South
Kentucky	Frankfort	Bluegrass State
Louisiana	Baton Rouge	Pelican State
Mississippi	Jackson	Magnolia State
North Carolina	Raleigh	Tar Heel State
South Carolina	Columbia	Palmetto State
Tennessee	Nashville	Volunteer State
Virginia	Richmond	Old Dominion
West Virginia	Charleston	Mountain State

The first people to inhabit the **SOUTHWEST** were the Pueblos. They are famous for building adobe structures out of sand, clay, water, and sticks. The Navajo came next, and then Spanish settlers. In the 1800s, the area was controlled by Mexico. Although the region is now a part of the United States, the Hispanic influence is still seen today in the region's language, religion, architecture, and food. In Oklahoma, in the 1930s, bad farming methods and a decade-long drought caused dust storms throughout the area giving it the nickname "the Dust Bowl."

The major industries of the Southwest include mining, technology, tourism, oil, and space travel. NASA opened its space center and mission control center, called the Lyndon B. Johnson Space Center, in Houston in 1961.

THE SOUTHWEST		
State	Capital	Nickname
Arizona	Phoenix	Grand Canyon State
Nevada	Carson City	Silver State
New Mexico	Santa Fe	Land of Enchantment
Oklahoma	Oklahoma City	Sooner State
Texas	Austin	Lone Star State

Follow the Colorado River north up into the **MOUNTAIN STATES** and the snowy Rocky Mountain range. Winter sports, such as skiing and snowboarding, are very popular here. Alta, a ski area near Salt Lake City, regularly gets more than 400 inches of snow each year!

THE MOUNTAIN STATES		
State	**Capital**	**Nickname**
Colorado	Denver	Centennial State
Idaho	Boise	Gem State
Montana	Helena	Treasure State
Utah	Salt Lake City	Beehive State
Wyoming	Cheyenne	Equality State

∽

Gold was first discovered in the **WEST** in California and Washington in the 1840s and 1850s and in Alaska in the 1890s. Once word got out, thousands of people hurried west as fast as they could, giving rise to the term *Gold Rush*. Many arrived in covered wagons, as the Transcontinental Railroad was not yet finished. This great migration transformed California's population, which grew by an estimated 86,000 people in the first two years of the Gold Rush. Today, California is the most populated state, with a larger economy than any other state.

THE WEST		
State	**Capital**	**Nickname**
Alaska	Juneau	The Last Frontier
California	Sacramento	Golden State
Hawaii	Honolulu	Aloha State
Oregon	Salem	Beaver State
Washington	Olympia	Evergreen State

∽

Alaska and Hawaii were the last two states to be admitted into the union. They both became states in 1959 and are the only two states that are not connected to the rest of the United States. Those are some of the only things they have in common.

SOPHOMORE YEAR: NORTH & SOUTH AMERICA

CANADA AND MEXICO

NORTH AMERICA is made up of Canada, the United States, Mexico, Central America, and the nations of the Caribbean.

∽

Some basic facts about **CANADA:**

- **CAPITAL:** Ottawa
- **AREA:** 3.8 million square miles
- **POPULATION:** 35.4 million
- **OFFICIAL LANGUAGES:** English and French

∽

CANADA is the second-largest country in the world by size. It reaches from the Atlantic Ocean to the Pacific Ocean and up to the Arctic Circle. Its only neighbor is the United States, with which it shares its southern and northwestern boundaries. Canada is known for its large lakes, cold winters, and great hockey teams.

∽

Canada is divided into regions like the United States, known as provinces. There are ten provinces in Canada: British Columbia, Alberta, Saskatchewan, Manitoba, Quebec, Ontario, New Brunswick, Prince Edward Island, Nova Scotia, Newfoundland, and Labrador. There are also three territories in Canada: Northwest Territories, Yukon, and Nunavut.

Some basic facts about **MEXICO**:

- **CAPITAL:** Mexico City
- **AREA:** 761,600 square miles
- **POPULATION:** 119 million
- **OFFICIAL LANGUAGE:** Spanish

MEXICO reaches from the Pacific Ocean to the Gulf of Mexico. It has dry deserts just like the American Southwest, but it also has some of the most beautiful cloud forests and rainforests in the world.

The **RÍO BRAVO DEL NORTE** (or as it's known English: the Rio Grande) is more than 1,000 miles long and forms the boundary between Mexico and part of Texas. The river starts in Colorado and empties into the Gulf of Mexico.

THE CARIBBEAN

The more than 7,000 **CARIBBEAN ISLANDS** that form an archipelago around the boundary of the Caribbean Sea are also formally a part of North America.

There are thirteen sovereign nations located in the Caribbean, as well as nineteen dependent territories ruled by the United Kingdom, France, the Netherlands, and the United States. The three largest island nations are Cuba, Jamaica, and Grenada.

CARIBBEAN NATIONS

Country	Capital	Official Language
Antigua and Barbuda	Saint John's	English
The Bahamas	Nassau	English
Barbados	Bridgetown	English
Cuba	Havana	Spanish
Dominica	Roseau	English
The Dominican Republic	Santo Domingo	Spanish
Grenada	Saint George's	English
Haiti	Port-au-Prince	French & Creole
Jamaica	Kingston	English
Saint Kitts and Nevis	Basseterre	English
Saint Lucia	Castries	English
Saint Vincent and the Grenadines	Kingstown	English
Trinidad and Tobago	Port of Spain	English

EXTRACURRICULARS: NEWSPAPER
THE GREAT HURRICANE OF 1780 HITS CARIBBEAN

Over six days in October 1780, a hurricane with winds that likely topped 200 mph, and considered the deadliest of all time, blasted through Barbados, Martinique, and Saint Lucia, killing more than 22,000 people, including American and British soldiers in warships as part of the Revolutionary War. It was not named as modern hurricanes are, but is known simply as **THE GREAT HURRICANE OF 1780**.

CENTRAL AMERICA

CENTRAL AMERICA is made up of the seven countries on the isthmus between North and South America.

ഗ

Central America is geologically active, meaning there have been many earthquakes and volcanoes. It is a region of the world known for its biodiversity as well.

ഗ

With the exception of Belize, where the official language is English, all Central American nations primarily speak Spanish.

CENTRAL AMERICA:		
Country	Capital	Population
Belize	Belmopan	340,844
Costa Rica	San José	4.8 million
El Salvador	San Salvador	6.1 million
Guatemala	Guatemala City	14.6 million
Honduras	Tegucigalpa	8.6 million
Nicaragua	Managua	5.8 million
Panama	Panama City	3.6 million

SOUTH AMERICA

SOUTH AMERICA stretches all the way from the equator to the South Pole. It is home to the largest rainforest on the planet and some of the highest, most treacherous mountains as well. Volcanoes dot the western boundary of South America, and rolling beaches are found on the eastern coast.

☞

Cape Horn marks the northern boundary of the Drake Passage. It is known for severe winds, harsh weather, and hazardous conditions. Before the **PANAMA CANAL** opened in 1914, sailors and traders trying to reach the Pacific Ocean from the Atlantic had to travel around South America, a dangerous path around Cape Horn. The Panama Canal provided shippers, sailors, and traders an alternate passage between the Atlantic and the Pacific.

☞

BRAZIL is the largest country in South America by size. It makes up just about half of the entire continent of South America! Brazil is located in the Northern Hemisphere, the Southern Hemisphere, and the Western Hemisphere.

☞

SURINAME is the continent's smallest country. It gained its independence from the Netherlands in 1975.

☞

South America holds several world's records for geography:

- World's largest river by volume: Amazon River
- World's highest waterfall: Angel Falls
- World's longest mountain range: the Andes
- World's driest desert: Atacama Desert
- World's biggest rainforest: Amazon rainforest
- World's southernmost town: Puerto Toro, Chile
- World's capital at highest elevation: La Paz, Bolivia

THE ANDES are found along the west coast of South America. They are more than 4,400 miles long, stretch as wide as 300 miles in places, and reach an average height of 13,000 feet above sea level. The Andes pass through seven of the twelve South American countries: Argentina, Chile, Peru, Bolivia, Venezuela, Columbia, and Ecuador.

SOUTH AMERICA		
Country	**Capital**	**Population**
Argentina	Buenos Aires	42.6 million
Bolivia	Sucre/La Paz	10 million
Brazil	Brasília	202 million
Chile	Santiago	17.7 million
Colombia	Bogotá	47.7 million
Ecuador	Quito	15.8 million
Guyana	Georgetown	784,894
Paraguay	Asunción	6.7 million
Peru	Lima	30.8 million
Suriname	Paramaribo	534,189
Uruguay	Montevideo	3.2 million
Venezuela	Caracas	30.2 million

JUNIOR YEAR: EUROPE & ASIA

EUROPE

Some basic facts about **EUROPE:**

- **COUNTRIES:** 50 sovereign states, 6 partially recognized territories
- **AREA:** 3.9 million square miles
- **POPULATION:** 742 million
- **LARGEST CITY:** Istanbul, Turkey (14 million)

∽

There are many ways to divide Europe, but here let's split them into three different regions: Western Europe, Eastern Europe, and the Mediterranean region.

∽

The countries of **WESTERN EUROPE** are typically near the coast of the Atlantic Ocean, and include: Andorra, Austria, Belgium, Denmark, Finland, France, Germany, Iceland, Ireland, Lichtenstein, Luxembourg, Malta, Monaco, the Netherlands, Norway, Portugal, San Marino, Spain, Sweden, Switzerland, and the United Kingdom.

∽

Western Europe has extremes in temperatures, climates, peoples, and cultures. The reaches of Norway and Sweden are covered in frozen tundra. Countries such as Portugal and Spain have beautiful, warm beaches along the shores of the Mediterranean Sea. Many of the other countries of Western Europe are covered by the Alps, one of the major mountain ranges in Europe. France and Spain are separated by the Pyrenees Mountains.

ಬಾ

The United Kingdom of Great Britain and Northern Ireland consists of four different kingdoms that are sometimes listed as individual countries. England, Scotland, Wales, and Northern Ireland together make up what we can call the United Kingdom.

ಬಾ

The landscape, boundaries, and names of the countries of **EASTERN EUROPE** have changed drastically over the decades. Today the countries include: Albania, Armenia, Azerbaijan, Belarus, Bosnia and Herzegovina, Bulgaria, the Czech Republic, Estonia, Georgia, Hungary, Kosovo, Latvia, Lithuania, Macedonia, Moldova, Montenegro, Poland, Romania, Russia, Slovakia, Slovenia, and Ukraine.

ಬಾ

Eastern Europe has several peninsulas that are all important to the geography of the region. The Balkan Peninsula juts out into the Mediterranean Sea. The Crimean and the Caucasus Peninsulas are surrounded by the Black Sea. Shipping and trade by water has always been important to the region.

৩

Moldova is one of Eastern Europe's most prosperous farming countries. The people of Moldova raise and export many different fruits and vegetables. People may be most familiar with Moldova for its vineyards—the wine industry in Moldova is quite large.

৩

Poland is home to more than 10,000 lakes. The highest peak in Poland is Rysy, which reaches more than 8,000 feet into the air.

৩

The countries of the **MEDITERRANEAN** region are where many of the world's ancient cultures and cities were born. These cities and cultures have grown to be today's modern countries, including Cyprus, Greece, and Italy

৩

The climate of the Mediterranean region is unique to the rest of Europe. The area has hot, dry summers and cool, wet winters. Mediterranean countries like Greece are known for growing and producing products like pine nuts, olives, and cheeses.

৩

The only active volcanoes on the mainland of Europe are found in Italy. One of the world's most infamous volcanoes, Mount Vesuvius, last erupted in 1944. This is the same volcano that erupted in the year 79 C.E. and buried the ancient cities of Pompeii and Herculaneum with a thick layer of ash. Mount Etna, located off the coast of the Italian island of Sicily, is the most active volcano in Europe.

ASIA

Some basic facts about **ASIA:**

- **COUNTRIES:** 49 sovereign states
- **AREA:** 17 million square miles
- **POPULATION:** 4.1 billion
- **LARGEST CITY:** Tokyo, Japan (33 million)

ω

THE MIDDLE EAST is the region of the world located near and around the Mediterranean Sea, and includes: Bahrain, Iran, Iraq, Israel, Jordan, Kuwait, Lebanon, Oman, Saudi Arabia, Syria, the United Arab Emirates, and Yemen.

ω

The Middle East is mainly known for its deserts, but there are also important bodies of water. The **TIGRIS RIVER** is about 1,180 miles long. It has its source in Turkey and then flows south until it meets up with the **EUPHRATES RIVER** in Iraq. From there, the two rivers continue as one until they reach the Persian Gulf. The Euphrates is about 1,700 miles long and it gets its water from the mountains of Turkey. The river rises when the snow melts every year.

ω

THE ARABIAN DESERT reaches from Yemen to Jordan. The temperatures can get pretty extreme, which makes it difficult for life to exist. Along the border between Saudi Arabia and Oman there is region of quicksand, which desert travelers need to look out for.

ω

CENTRAL ASIA is home to the "stans"—Afghanistan, Kazakhstan, Kyrgyzstan, Tajikistan, Turkmenistan, and Uzbekistan.

The second largest country in Asia is **INDIA**. It has an area of 1.27 million square miles, and is home to more than 1.2 billion people. Only China has more people, with 1.3 billion.

Along with India, the other countries in **SOUTH ASIA** are: Bangladesh, Bhutan, Maldives, Nepal, Pakistan, and Sri Lanka.

The nations of **SOUTHEAST ASIA** are separated into two groups. The mainland countries are Cambodia, Laos, Myanmar, Thailand, and Vietnam, while the island nations include: Brunei, East Timor, Indonesia, Malaysia, the Philippines, and Singapore.

The final group of nations is known as **EAST ASIA**, and includes China, Japan, North Korea, and South Korea.

CHINA shares its border with fifteen other nations, and its climate ranges from tropical in the southern parts to subarctic in the north.

JAPAN is made up of thousands of tiny islands and four main islands: Hokkaido, Honshu, Kyushu, and Shikoku. Located on Honshu Island, Mount Fuji is the nation's highest peak and a sacred place in Japan.

The Korean Peninsula includes both **NORTH KOREA** and **SOUTH KOREA**, two vastly different nations. The capital of North Korea is Pyongyang, and the capital of South Korea is Seoul.

SENIOR YEAR: AFRICA & OCEANIA

AFRICA

Some basic facts about **AFRICA:**

- **COUNTRIES:** 54 sovereign states
- **AREA:** 30 million square miles
- **POPULATION:** 1.1 billion
- **LARGEST CITY:** Lagos, Nigeria (8 million)

Africa is the second largest continent in the world, and its landscape ranges from vast deserts to dense rainforests, from grassy savannas to snowy mountain ranges. Africa is home to many of the biggest and best-known wild animals on Earth—lions, zebras, giraffes, crocodiles, hippopotamuses, chimpanzees, gorillas, lemurs, and more.

ഗ

Africa is bordered by the Atlantic Ocean on the west and the Indian Ocean on the east, the Mediterranean Sea to the north, and the Suez Canal and the Red Sea to the northeast. Africa is considered to be the oldest inhabited area on Earth. In the middle of the 1900s, anthropologists found fossils and artifacts on this continent that showed human life at least 7 million years ago.

ഗ

NORTH AFRICA, which borders the Mediterranean and which is also considered a part of the Middle East, includes: Algeria, Egypt, Libya, Morocco, and Tunisia.

EGYPT consists mostly of a large desert with a long river flowing through it. Most people in the country live close to the **NILE RIVER**, the world's longest, which is 4,160 miles total.

∽

Northeastern Africa is often referred to as the *Horn of Africa* because of its geographic shape. Djibouti, Eritrea, Ethiopia, Somalia, and Sudan make up the region, which is bordered by the Red Sea and the Gulf of Aden.

∽

The **SAHARA DESERT** covers the northern part of the continent, and stretches across twelve countries, or about a quarter of Africa. The landforms are shaped by the wind and the sand. The area receives less than 10 inches of rain per year. (By contrast, Seattle receives nearly 40 inches per year.)

∽

Just below the Sahara in **WEST AFRICA**, is the Sahel, an area of biological and environmental transition between the desert and the grasslands and savanna just to the south. To the east in Central Africa, you'll find rainforests and the **GREAT RIFT VALLEY**, which runs 3,700 miles from Lebanon to Mozambique and is made up of separate valleys and fault lines that include the Rift Valley Lakes, such as Lake Tanganyika, and is where scientists have found some of the earliest human bones and artifacts.

∽

In **SOUTHERN AFRICA**, through Tanzania and Zambia, the **NAMIB** and **KALAHARI** deserts dominate the landscape, adjacent to the tropical forests and grassy plains.

The southernmost point of Africa, in South Africa, is called **THE CAPE OF GOOD HOPE**. It was a frequent spot for ships to sail around en route from Europe to India and the East.

SOUTH AFRICA'S largest city is Johannesburg, and it has three capitals: Pretoria is the administrative capital; Bloemfontein the judicial; and Cape Town, the legislative.

Within South Africa's borders there are two small landlocked nations: **LESOTHO** and **SWAZILAND**. Both are former British colonies and received their independence in the 1960s.

The large island off the coast of eastern Africa, and the fourth largest island in the world, is called **MADAGASCAR**. Because of its isolation, the island has many different kinds of plant and animal species found nowhere else in the world.

The region of the world that contains Australia, New Zealand, Papua New Guinea, and the rest of the Pacific island nations is **OCEANIA**.

EXTRACURRICULARS: STUDENT COUNCIL

SOUTH SUDAN, the world's youngest nation, became independent from Sudan in 2011, through a referendum that passed with more than 98 percent of the vote.

OCEANIA

Some basic facts about **OCEANIA:**

- **COUNTRIES:** 14 sovereign states
- **AREA:** 8.5 million square miles
- **POPULATION:** 36 million
- **LARGEST CITY:** Sydney, Australia (3.7 million)

∽

AUSTRALIA is split into six states: New South Wales, Queensland, South Australia, Tasmania, Victoria, and Western Australia. The capital is Canberra.

∽

Located off the northeastern edge of Australia in the Coral Sea is the **GREAT BARRIER REEF.** It's about 1,600 miles long, is made up of nearly 3,000 individual reefs, and contains more than 400 kinds of coral and 1,500 species of fish. Coral are living organisms, so it is the largest structure in the world built by living creatures.

EXTRACURRICULARS: DRAMA CLUB

The **SYDNEY OPERA HOUSE** is by far one of the most iconic theaters in the world. The building, which features a modern expressionist design, opened in 1973, and serves as a concert hall and theater for world-class performances.

∽

The Maori name for **NEW ZEALAND** is Aotearoa, which means "land of the long white cloud."

The largest city in New Zealand is Auckland, and the capital is Wellington.

There are between 20,000 and 30,000 islands in the Pacific Ocean—some are high islands with volcanic, fertile soil, and others are low islands or reefs.

The people who live on these islands are usually Melanesian, Micronesian, or Polynesian.

PAPUA NEW GUINEA, located on New Guinea island and its off-shore islands in Melanesia, is one of the most multicultural nations in the world with more than 850 cultures and languages.

FIJI is a group of 322 islands and 533 islets. The capital and largest city is Suva.

A part of Micronesia, the **MARSHALL ISLANDS** are made up of twenty-nine atolls and five separate islands. The capital and largest city is Majuro.

PERIOD 4
HISTORY

THEY SAY THAT YOU NEED TO KNOW WHERE YOU'VE BEEN TO HAVE A SENSE OF WHERE YOU'RE GOING. But the real reason to study history is to see that humans keep making the same mistakes over and over again. The only way to break the pattern is to truly try to be exceptional. So study up on the history of the world, and try to find ways to apply these lessons to an exceptional life.

FRESHMAN YEAR: ANCIENT HISTORY

EARLY CIVILIZATIONS

Six thousand years ago, the first civilizations developed between the **TIGRIS** and **EUPHRATES** Rivers in what is now Iraq. The first civilization was known as **SUMER**, and the different villages developed self-governing city-states with a temple, or ziggurat, at the center of each city-state. A hot, dry climate combined with seasonal flooding to produce very fertile soil, which farmers took advantage of, cultivating crops such as wheat, barley, sesame, and flax.

∽

The **ZIGGURAT** at the heart of each city-state served many purposes. Not only were they there for religious reasons, but they were also the center of daily life for the Sumerian people. The Sumerians believed there were many powerful gods in the sky, and they dedicated these large temples to them. The ziggurats were built of mud-brick, with steps leading to the top, where religious ceremonies were held.

∽

The **AKKADIANS** were a Semitic people from the Arabian Peninsula who increasingly came into more conflict with the Sumerians as they migrated north. In 2340 B.C.E. Sargon, the Akkadian military leader, conquered Sumerian city-states and established an Akkadian empire over the land. Sargon established his rule in the city of Akkad, and created the largest empire known to man at that time. The empire was short-lived, and in 2125 B.C.E. the Akkadian Empire fell.

As the last Sumerian dynasty fell, the Amorites came to power, basing their capital in **BABYLON**. One of the most notable legal texts in history comes from this time period, when the king, **HAMMURABI**, created one of the first set of written laws. This is called the Code of Hammurabi. These laws were written out so that all would know the punishments if they disobeyed them. One of the most famous paraphrases of this code is "An eye for an eye, and a tooth for a tooth."

No one knows the origins of the **HITTITES**, and until recently, their language was undecipherable (it was in the Indo-European family). Their invasion brought the end of the Old Babylonian Empire; however, as they conquered **MESOPOTAMIA**, they adopted the laws, literature, and religion of Old Babylon. The Hittites are most notable for their work in trade and commerce, which spread Mesopotamian literature and thought throughout the Mediterranean.

EXTRACURRICULARS: DRAMA CLUB

THE FLINTSTONES, a cartoon series about a "modern stone age family," ran for six seasons on ABC in the 1960s. It is often cited as one of the greatest cartoon series of all time. It followed a family of cave people several thousand years before Mesopotamia developed.

Many important inventions came out of Mesopotamia. The seeder plow was revolutionary in agriculture and allowed seeding and plowing to occur simultaneously. The people of Mesopotamia also created a writing system based on images called cuneiform, developed irrigation and sanitation methods, created glass, and around 3500 B.C.E., invented the wheel. They were also the first to harness wind energy by creating sails.

ANCIENT EGYPT

EGYPT's history began similarly to that of Mesopotamia. Civilizations congregated around the **NILE RIVER** around 5500 B.C.E. The largest civilization, the Badari, inhabited the northern part of Egypt, and was most known for high-quality stone tools, ceramics and pottery, and their use of copper. In the southern part of Egypt, the Naqada civilization arose. Over the course of 1,000 years, the Naqada controlled the tribes along the Nile, and created a full system of **HIEROGLYPHICS** for writing.

ᨦ

Around 3100 B.C.E., Upper and Lower Egypt united under the pharaoh Menes. Memphis, a part of Lower Egypt, was established as the capital of the land and became critical in trade and agriculture. It also provided a work force. Notable from this time period were the mastaba tombs, which were large rectangular, flat-roofed structures made of stone and mud bricks that were built to celebrate pharaohs who had died.

ᨦ

The **OLD KINGDOM** refers to the rule of the Third Dynasty to the Sixth Dynasty from 2686 to 2181 B.C.E. This was a time defined by a flourishing economy, a well-defined justice system, and a strong government. It is during this time that the famous pyramids of Giza were built, marking great artistic and technological advancements.

ᨦ

The central government of the Old Kingdom collapsed in 2160 B.C.E., and around 2055 B.C.E., the prosperity and stability of Egypt was restored when Mentuhotep II came to power beginning what is known as the Middle Kingdom. Once again, art, literature, and great monuments defined the period. One stark contrast between the art of this time and that of the Old Kingdom, is that the work focused more on the individual and a democratization of the afterlife in which every person possessed a soul and was greeted by the gods and goddesses when they died.

∽

The **NEW KINGDOM** lasted from the sixteenth to the eleventh century B.C.E. and was defined by military campaigns that made the Egyptian Empire the largest it had ever been. Amenhotep IV, who changed his name to Akhenaten, instituted new and radical worship of a new sun god, Aten. Attacking the priestly establishment, Akhenaten eventually made Aten the only god. When Tutankhamen came to power after Akhenaten's death, he returned Egypt to a polytheistic religion.

∽

The **LATE PERIOD** lasted from 664 to 323 B.C.E. It is considered to be the end of the once great Egyptian Empire. From 525 to 404 B.C.E., Egypt was part of the Persian Empire. The Twenty-eighth Dynasty, led by Amyrtaeus, saw a revolt against the Persians; however, by the Thirtieth Dynasty in 343 B.C.E., the Persians had once again reoccupied the land.

ANCIENT ROME

According to legend, **ROMULUS** and **REMUS** were the children of the god Mars. Mars feared they would one day kill him, and decided to drown them. They were rescued by a she-wolf and raised by her until ultimately being found by a shepherd and his wife. When the boys grew older, they decided to build a city. In a fight over who would rule the city, Romulus killed Remus with a rock. Romulus then named the city after himself, calling it **ROME**.

∽

The **ROMAN KINGDOM** lasted from 753 to 509 B.C.E. Rome was established as a village on the Tiber River and was ruled by seven kings (with Romulus as the first), who were elected by the village to serve for life. According to legend, Romulus's followers were mostly men from all classes, including slaves, and the shortage of women brought about the abduction of women from the neighboring tribe, the Sabines. The Kingdom of Rome expanded to 350 square miles at this time. Most notably, a Senate of 100 men was created to act as an advisory council to the king.

∽

After the last king, **TARQUIN THE PROUD**, was overthrown, a republican system based on elected magistrates was put into effect, and along with the Senate, there was a new focus on separation of powers and a system of checks and balances. The Roman Republic lasted from 500 to 30 B.C.E. During this time, Rome expanded throughout the Mediterranean and into North Africa, Greece, and the Iberian Peninsula. Toward the end of this time period, one of the most famous rulers, Julius Caesar, came to power and attempted to become a dictator of Rome.

∽

The Roman Empire, which lasted from 27 B.C.E. to 1453 C.E., began when **OCTAVIAN** took control of the empire after **JULIUS CAESAR** was assassinated by a group of senators. The republic was never re-established, as the emperor held most of the power, but the Senate continued. Rome continued to expand, and by the time Trajan ruled

(98–117 C.E.), the Roman Empire had expanded 6.5 million square kilometers. To better control the vast empire, authority was divided between four co-emperors. These divisions would ultimately divide the Roman Empire into a Western Empire and an Eastern Empire.

∽

The Western Empire of Rome collapsed in 476 C.E. with an attack from the Visigoths. In 1453, the Eastern Empire collapsed, thus ending the great Roman Empire. There were several contributing factors that led to the fall of Rome, including its grand size, making it hard to control its people; the influence and spread of the newly formed religion, Christianity; the spread of Islam; attacks from barbarians; inflation; and even lead poisoning.

∽

Construction of the **COLOSSEUM**, one of the best-known monumental structures associated with Rome, began in 72 C.E. and was completed eight years later. The amphitheater could seat 55,000 spectators and was 159 feet tall. Free games were held in the Colosseum for the public, representing power and prestige, and the events included comedy acts and gladiatorial fights to the death with animals and other gladiators.

THE OTTOMAN EMPIRE

The **OTTOMAN EMPIRE** arose in the early fourteenth century, just as the Roman Empire began to fall. It was originally created when the empire of the Seljuk Turks broke down. As the Ottomans began absorbing other states, by the reign of Muhammad II in 1451, all local Turkish dynasties had ended. Under Osman I and subsequent rulers, many attacks were aimed at the Byzantine Empire.

From the reign of Muhammad II onward, the Ottoman Empire expanded widely over the land. In 1453, the Ottomans took over **CONSTANTINOPLE**, the capital of the Byzantine Empire. Expansion of the Ottoman Empire reached its peak in the sixteenth century under Sultan Selim I and Süleyman I. The empire expanded to include Hungary, Transylvania, Persia, Egypt, Syria, and Greece.

One of the reasons the Ottoman Empire was so successful was its ability to unify a wide variety of people through its tolerance of other religions. This was done by establishing **MILLETS**. Millets were religious groups of people that were able to practice and retain their own laws, language, and traditions of their religions. The many different ethnicities, however, led to a weakness in nationalism, one of the contributing factors of the empire's decline.

From the sixteenth to the eighteenth century, the Ottoman Empire faced many wars, rebellions, and treaties. This took a great toll on the empire economically. The Ottoman Empire would come to lose control of Serbia, Montenegro, Bosnia, Romania, Herzegovina, Greece, and Egypt. The once flourishing Turkey was now being referred to as "the Sick Man of Europe."

In 1908, a nationalist and reformist group called the **YOUNG TURKS** forced the restoration of the 1876 constitution. In 1909, the sultan was deposed by Parliament and replaced by Muhammad V. In the two Balkan Wars, Turkey lost nearly all of its European territory. During World War I, Turkey aligned with the Central Powers, and in 1918, the resistance collapsed, thus ending the Ottoman Empire.

SOPHOMORE YEAR: MODERN WORLD HISTORY

THE MAGNA CARTA

In 1215, the Magna Carta was created. To this day, it is still one of the most celebrated documents ever written. Literally meaning "Great Charter," the Magna Carta consisted of thirty-seven laws that greatly reduced the power of the king and allowed for the formation of **PARLIAMENT**. King John of England was forced to sign the document.

∽

A large section of the Magna Carta is referred to today as **CLAUSE 61**. This established the creation of a committee composed of twenty-five barons who would have the power to overcome the rule of the king at any time should he defy what was written in the charter. If necessary, these barons could seize the king's possessions and castles. Both King John and the pope refused to allow this, and England entered into a civil war, known as the First Barons' War. The Magna Carta was only valid for three months, and was considered to be a failure.

∽

Today, only three of the original sixty-three clauses are still valid in England. The first clause guaranteed the liberties of the Church of England. The second clause declared that London and all of the other cities, towns, ports, and boroughs would be allowed to enjoy their ancient customs and liberties. The last clause, and the best-known of the three, states that no free man shall be imprisoned, seized, or stripped of his rights except by a lawful judgment by his equals and that no one will be denied justice.

The Magna Carta greatly influenced the United States Constitution, the Declaration of Independence, and the Bill of Rights during the writing of these documents. The third clause from the Magna Carta, which states accused persons shall not be imprisoned until found guilty by their peers is perhaps the most obvious influence, as it appears in the Fifth Amendment of the Bill of Rights. Also, the first clause included the principle of the separation of church and state.

> **EXTRACURRICULARS: STUDENT COUNCIL**
> Nearly 800 years after the signing of the Magna Carta, the Treaty of Lisbon officially established the European Union (EU), as we know it today, as well as a European Parliament made up of member states from the region, to look after the collective interests of the area. As of 2014, there were twenty-eight member states in the EU.

THE RENAISSANCE

The **RENAISSANCE** was a return to the classicism and humanism of ancient Greece in Europe following the Middle Ages. Following the Black Death, there was a great change in the European economy. That, along with the invention of the printing press, the fall of the Byzantine Empire, and the Crusades all led to the birth of the Renaissance, where classic Greek and Roman art, literature, and philosophy were reintroduced into European culture.

The Renaissance began in Florence, Italy. Much of the great artwork in the early Renaissance can be traced back to a family of the noble class, the **MEDICI** family. In the fourteenth century, the Medici acquired great wealth as bankers and became the wealthiest family in all of Italy. With their wealth, they sponsored many artistic endeavors, such as the great paintings and architecture of this time.

ιon

The early Renaissance was from 1330 to 1450, and took place in Florence, Italy. Artwork sponsored by the Medici family placed great focus on the art of ancient Greece and Rome. The artwork once again focused on humanism, naturalism, and realism, with new ideas introduced into art such as depth of field, linear perspective, and new types of shading. The best-known artists to come out of the early Renaissance are Sandro Botticelli (*Primavera*), Domenico Ghirlandaio (*Portrait of an Old Man and His Grandson*), and Piero della Francesca (*Baptism of Christ*).

ιon

The artwork of the **HIGH RENAISSANCE**, which was from 1490 to 1530, made advances on the techniques of artists of the early Renaissance. The center of the High Renaissance was Rome, and artwork was now being commissioned by the popes. It is during the High Renaissance that the best-known works of Renaissance painters appeared. The best-known artists to come out of the High Renaissance are Leonardo da Vinci (*The Last Supper*), Michelangelo Buonarroti (*The Creation of Adam*), and Raphael (*Sistine Madonna*).

ιon

The Northern Renaissance was from 1500 to 1600, and it took place outside of Italy. The ideas of the Renaissance quickly spread throughout Europe, and some of the most notable artwork of the time came from the Netherlands and Germany. This artwork is distinctively different from the work produced in Italy, due to the increasing disenchantment with the church. The figures appeared less classical, and more realistic. The best-known artists to come out of the Northern Renaissance are the Flemish painter Jan van Eyck (*The Arnolfini Portrait*), the German painter Albrecht Dürer (*Knight, Death, and the Devil*), and the Dutch painter Hieronymus Bosch (*Garden of Earthly Delights*).

ભ

It was during the Renaissance period that the first portable clocks, eyeglasses, printing press, microscope, telescope, and even the first flush toilet were created. With the rise of technology and science, ideas such as gravity and the ability to study the universe led to the notion that the universe was not simply centered on mankind.

THE MIDDLE AGES

The early Middle Ages, also known as the **DARK AGES**, followed the collapse of the Western Roman Empire, and lasted from the fifth century to the tenth century. From 400 to 700 C.E., Europe was greatly divided, and there was a great migration of Germanic and Slavic people. Along with the increase in migration, this time period was marked by an economic decline. Many empires rose and fell during this time, never being able to achieve the status or success of the Roman Empire. It is also during this time that feudalism starts to appear.

ભ

The High Middle Ages, which lasted from the eleventh to the thirteenth century, was defined by **URBANIZATION**, a unifying religion in **CHRISTIANITY**, and a rise in population and military expansion. It is during this time that the **CRUSADES**, a series of wars fought between Christians and Muslims over the Holy Land occurred. From the Crusades came contact with Arab science, math, and philosophy, which had been developed from the classical works of ancient Greek philosophers. The contributions made by the Muslim world were passed on to Europe.

The late Middle Ages, which lasted from 1300 to 1500, was a time defined by climate change, famine, disease, war, and social upheaval. **THE GREAT FAMINE** of 1315 to 1317 and the Black Death led to an incredibly large loss of life. It is during this time that the **HUNDRED YEARS' WAR** was fought between England and France, and it is in the late Middle Ages that the schism in the Catholic Church occurs.

In 1347, Europe was struck by the **BLACK DEATH** (now known to have been the bubonic plague). It is believed that one-third to one-half of the entire population of Europe was killed by this plague. The common belief is that rats in ships arriving from Asia were infected with the disease. The disease then moved from rats to fleas, and then the fleas would bite humans, infecting them. From there, the disease spread from human to human.

There were many major technological advances made during the Middle Ages. Among the most important inventions were the use of gunpowder, vertical windmills, the mechanical clock, the printing press, eyeglasses, and improvements on water mills. Advancements were made in agriculture as well, with the introduction of the heavy plough and three-field crop rotation.

THE REFORMATION

By the beginning of the sixteenth century, Roman Catholicism was the only religion in Western Europe. The church believed that it alone had the power to interpret the Bible. However, with the

Renaissance and the invention of the printing press, people started believing the church had too much control. In the fourteenth century, a man named John Wycliffe became the first to translate the Bible from Latin into English. This idea was soon picked up by Jan Hus of Bohemia, who began preaching his own sermons.

∽

In 1517, **MARTIN LUTHER**, an Augustinian monk, became fed up with the church's policies of selling indulgences and misleading people. Luther wrote the **NINETY-FIVE THESES ON THE POWER AND EFFICACY OF INDULGENCES** against the practices of the church, as well as new ideas for a better religion (such as rejecting the authority of the pope). Luther nailed his Ninety-Five Theses on the door of the church at Wittenberg.

∽

At the same time that Luther's ideas began to spread, **ULRICH ZWINGLI** led a similar revolt in Switzerland. The printing press enabled the ideas of Luther and Zwingli to reach the general public; however, there were differences in some of their ideologies. The teachings of Luther would become established as Lutheranism. Soon another voice would rise and become a prominent figure in the **PROTESTANT REFORMATION**: John Calvin.

∽

In 1536, **JOHN CALVIN**, a lawyer, published *The Institutes of the Christian Religion*, in which he expressed his theology. Calvin's teachings gained in popularity, and soon Calvin would reform the church in Geneva and force its citizens to follow his practices. Although Calvin and Luther were contemporaries and shared many similar beliefs, there were considerable differences. In particular, Calvinism espoused the idea of predestination, that a person was destined at birth to either be saved or doomed to damnation.

On October 18, 1584, citizens of Paris awoke to find the city covered with placards denouncing the Catholic Mass and condemning the Eucharist, among other things. These placards were also posted all around northern France and even on the king's door. A group of **HUGUENOTS**, French adherents of Calvinism, were deemed the culprits, and were burned. Suppression of Protestantism soon followed.

Initially, the Catholic Church thought nothing of the Reformation, but as it spread from country to country, the church established the Council of Trent to repair the schism that was occurring. A Spanish nobleman named Ignatius of Loyola, who had renounced his military life, founded the Jesuits, a group that made reforms from within the church. By the end of the sixteenth century, half of the lands lost to Protestant reform returned to the Catholic Church, a divide that still exists today.

CHRISTOPHER COLUMBUS

CHRISTOPHER COLUMBUS spent much of his life sailing the Atlantic Ocean. He became very interested in traveling to the Far East, which he believed was just across the Atlantic Ocean. His idea was to create a sea route to India and attain the gold and spices of the East Indies. Columbus met with King John II of Portugal to support his journey, but was soon rejected. He then met with the monarchs of Spain, King Ferdinand and Queen Isabella, who, although they had rejected him initially, eventually agreed to support his journey.

Columbus prepared three ships, the **NIÑA**, the **PINTA**, and the **SANTA MARÍA**, for the journey. On August 3, 1492, they set sail.

On October 12, he landed on what is now the island of San Salvador in the Bahamas and took possession of the island. Columbus soon found Cuba (which he believed to be China), and in December, he reached Hispaniola (which Columbus believed to be Japan), and established a colony of thirty-nine men. In March of 1493, Columbus returned to Spain with riches, spices, and "Indian" captives.

や

Over the course of a century, the population of natives on the island of Hispaniola was completely destroyed in a genocide brought on by the Spanish. In 1493, policies regarding slavery and mass extermination were implemented, and within a three-year time span, 5 million Native Americans were killed. Mass numbers of Native Americans were hanged, stabbed, shot, and worked to death as slaves.

JUNIOR YEAR: U.S. HISTORY

THE AMERICAN REVOLUTION

It is unknown which side the **"SHOT HEARD 'ROUND THE WORLD"** came from, but on April 19, 1775, the British troops and the American colonists fought the first battle of the **REVOLUTIONARY WAR**. A rumor was circulating that the Massachusetts Militia had been storing weapons in Concord, and 700 British soldiers were sent to quell their mission. The colonists quickly learned of the oncoming British troops, leading to Paul Revere's famous horseback ride. Though both sides faced casualties, more British soldiers were left dead or wounded.

Following the **BATTLE OF LEXINGTON** and **CONCORD**, the colonists besieged Boston from the surrounding hills. When they heard news of the British planning to attack Bunker Hill and Breed's Hill, the colonists sent 1,600 militiamen to set up fortifications. On June 17, 1775, 2,600 British soldiers attacked. Most of the fighting took place on Breed's Hill. By the third charge from the British, the colonists had to retreat, and though the British gained control of Breed's Hill, they suffered a great amount of losses and casualties.

The evacuation of the British from Boston was a very important victory for the colonists, and also the first victory for **GENERAL GEORGE WASHINGTON**. As a result of the Battle of Bunker Hill, though the British won, they desperately needed reinforcements. To support Washington, Henry Knox, the chief artillery officer, brought fifty cannons from Fort Ticonderoga and positioned them to aim at the British fleet in Boston Harbor. On March 5, 1776, the British general saw the cannons aimed at them and took his men to Halifax, Canada.

Following a defeat, General George Washington decided to plan a surprise attack on the British and Hessian soldiers on Christmas day of 1776. Washington led 2,500 soldiers across the **DELAWARE RIVER** in a great snowstorm under treacherous conditions to reach Trenton, New Jersey. While the British soldiers slept, Washington and his men attacked, taking 1,000 prisoners and killing over 100 men without a single American killed.

The **BATTLE OF SARATOGA** is considered to be one of the major victories in the Revolutionary War and a turning point for the Americans.

The British army wished to control the Hudson River and cut New England off from the other colonies. British troops had planned to join with other troops along the way to quell the colonists; however, intervention from the Americans prevented this. On September 19, 1777, the first battle of Saratoga occurred, and on October 7, the second battle occurred, resulting in the surrender of the British troops.

∽

Though the **BATTLE OF YORKTOWN** did not end the American Revolution, it was the last major battle fought. On September 5, 1781, the French fleet arrived and defeated the British navy. The British general, Lord Cornwallis, found his men trapped between the American colonists and the French, and on October 19, 1781, he and his 8,000 troops surrendered. The surrender had a huge impact on the British government, as the war was being lost.

THE DECLARATION OF INDEPENDENCE AND THE CONSTITUTION

Before the Constitution was ever written, the **DECLARATION OF INDEPENDENCE** needed to be drafted, declaring the colonies' freedom from the British. The **CONTINENTAL CONGRESS** met in the summer of 1776 to discuss the writing of the important document, and on June 11, **THOMAS JEFFERSON** began the first draft. The final draft was submitted to the Continental Congress on June 28, and by July 2, the Continental Congress took a vote regarding their independence. On **JULY 4**, the document was released to the public.

∽

Upon winning their freedom, the thirteen states began to operate under their own rules, and a centralized government was strongly opposed out of fear that another monarchy could arise. As a compromise, the **ARTICLES OF CONFEDERATION** were drafted in 1776 and ratified in 1781. Essentially, this was the country's first constitution. Each state would retain its freedom, and a committee of representatives—a **CONGRESS**—would be responsible for declaring war, dealing with foreign affairs, and maintaining an army and navy. Though the document had a lot of good ideas, it had many short-comings, and these led to the creation of the Constitution.

ဟ

In 1787, the delegates from all of the states except Rhode Island met in Philadelphia to create a more centralized government. Two plans, the Virginia Plan and the New Jersey Plan, were presented. The **VIR-GINIA PLAN** consisted of a powerful centralized government that had executive, legislative, and judicial branches. The **NEW JERSEY PLAN** would make changes to the Articles of Confederation and allow Congress to control taxes and trade to some degree. A compro-mise was reached, combining parts of both plans.

ဟ

Currently, the Constitution has a preamble, seven original articles, a list of twenty-seven amendments, and a certification from the Constitutional Convention. The first article establishes the legisla-tive branch, defining Congress as a bicameral body with a House of Representatives and a Senate. Article II establishes the role of the presidency. Article III describes how the court system will work, and includes the Supreme Court.

ဟ

The **BILL OF RIGHTS** is the first ten amendments made to the Constitution. These amendments establish the specific rights every American citizen has. The Bill of Rights was created to calm the fears of Anti-Federalists who were wary of the Constitution and feared the presidency could turn into a monarchy. These rights include the freedom of speech and religion, the right to bear arms, and the right to have a fair trial by a jury.

☙

During the writing of the Constitution, the framers were aware that over time, certain changes would be necessary, and included the ability to amend the constitution. There have only been twenty-seven amendments to the U.S. Constitution. Some of the best-known are the Thirteenth Amendment, which abolished slavery; the Nineteenth Amendment, which established women's suffrage; and the Eighteenth Amendment, which prohibited the sale of alcohol. The Eighteenth Amendment was repealed by the Twenty-first Amendment.

THE WAR OF 1812

THE WAR OF 1812 began in 1812 and lasted until 1815. The British, warring with France, wanted to restrict trade between the newly formed United States of America and France. This was considered illegal by the Americans. Following years of Britain's restrictions and attacks on American ships, as well as their funding Native Americans' attacks on American settlements, war was declared on Britain and their Canadian colonies. This new war with Britain reaffirmed the stance that the United States had to be independent from Britain.

☙

When war was declared against the British, the **WAR HAWKS** (members of Congress who wanted to go to war with Britain and the Native Americans) set their sights on an attack of the British in Canada. The American forces divided into segments at Niagara, Lake Champlain, and Detroit. On July 12, 1812, the Americans invaded. The divided American troops were no match for the British, and fighting was pushed into American territory.

On December 14, 1814, Federalist delegates from Massachusetts, Connecticut, Vermont, New Hampshire, and Rhode Island met to discuss opposition to the war, and even the possibility of New England seceding. As a result of the Hartford Convention, constitutional amendments were proposed. These amendments stated that war and laws that restricted Congress needed a two-thirds majority in Congress, successive presidents could not be from the same state, presidents were limited to a single term, and the three-fifths clause would be eliminated.

The War of 1812 ended on December 24, 1814, with the signing of the **TREATY OF GHENT** between the United States and Britain. The treaty called for amnesty for all Native American participants, the return of prisoners of war and territory, the return of slaves, and a commitment to end the international slave trade.

Two weeks after the Treaty of Ghent, news of the treaty had not yet spread to the United States, and the United States fought in the Battle of New Orleans, its greatest military victory of the war. The British were 7,500 strong, while the Americans were only 5,000. A total of 2,036 British soldiers were killed, with only 21 American casualties, turning **ANDREW JACKSON**, the general of the battle, into a national hero.

THE CIVIL WAR

Before **ABRAHAM LINCOLN** even took office as president of the United States, the state of South Carolina perceived his election as a threat and called all state delegates to a meeting. The delegates voted to remove South Carolina from the United States in December of 1860. Mississippi, Alabama, Florida, Louisiana, Georgia, and Texas followed South Carolina's move, forming the **CONFEDERATE STATES OF AMERICA** on February 4, 1861. Four more states, Virginia, Tennessee, Arkansas, and North Carolina would join the Confederate States of America.

§

Though the events at **FORT SUMTER** started the Civil War, the first major battle was at **BULL RUN** on July 21, 1861. As pressure to crush the rebellion in the South grew, the Union army started to march toward Richmond, Virginia, the capital of the Confederacy. The Union army and the Confederate army met at Manassas. Though initially losing, the Confederates had reinforcements and Union soldiers began withdrawing. It was thought at the time that this would be the only battle of the war; however, as the battle came to a close, many came to the realization that this war was going to last much longer.

§

The **BATTLE OF SHILOH** is known as one the deadliest battles of the Civil War. Approximately 23,750 soldiers were killed or wounded, 13,000 being from the Union side. The Confederate army attacked **GENERAL ULYSSES S. GRANT**'s soldiers by surprise at Pittsburg Landing in Shiloh, Tennessee, on April 6, 1862. Though not prepared, the Union army was able to fight until reinforcements could come. The next day, Grant led a counterattack, forcing the Confederates to retreat and securing a victory for the Union.

§

In September of 1862, a preliminary form of the **EMANCIPATION PROCLAMATION** was ordered declaring that any slaves in the Confederate states would be freed unless the states rejoined the Union by January 1. The Confederate states did not take the offer, and on

January 1, 1863, President Lincoln issued the Emancipation Proclamation, stating that slaves in all the states would be granted freedom. The Emancipation Proclamation did not actually free all slaves however. Rather, it freed the slaves who were living in the Confederate states and allowed blacks to fight for the Union. Though ending slavery was never a major goal of the Civil War, the Emancipation Proclamation turned it into one.

ᗯᑎ

On November 19, 1863, President Lincoln issued one of the most famous speeches in American history: the **GETTYSBURG ADDRESS**. The speech was delivered in Gettysburg, Pennsylvania, four and a half months after the Battle of Gettysburg, where the Union had defeated the Confederates. The speech paid tribute to all lost soldiers, and featured no hatred or ill will, but emphasized the principles of democracy.

EXTRACURRICULARS: NEWSPAPER
PRESIDENT LINCOLN ASSASSINATED

On April 15, 1865, President Abraham Lincoln died from a gunshot wound that occurred the previous evening while attending a production of *Our American Cousin* at Ford's Theatre in Washington, DC. His assailant, actor John Wilkes Booth fled the city and was found twelve days later. He refused to surrender and was shot by a Union soldier. Booth and his conspirators were unsuccessfully attempting to revive the Confederate cause.

ᗯᑎ

In the spring of 1865 Confederate **GENERAL ROBERT E. LEE** fled with his army to Appomattox County with Grant's army in pursuit. Seven days after the capture of Richmond, on April 9, 1865, Lee knew that Grant would win another battle, and decided to meet with Grant at Appomattox Court House. The two men showed great respect for each other, and Robert E. Lee surrendered. Though this did not end the war immediately, the loss of Robert E. Lee's army would lead to the surrender of the other Confederate armies.

SENIOR YEAR: CONTEMPORARY HISTORY

WORLD WAR I

On June 28, 1914, **ARCHDUKE FRANZ FERDINAND**, heir to the Austro-Hungarian Empire, was assassinated by a member of the Serbian terrorist group known as the Black Hand. This event would lead to the beginning of the Great War. Following the murder, the government of Austria-Hungary had to impose their authority on Serbia, and they called on Germany for support. On July 23, an ultimatum was delivered to Serbia to wipe out terrorist groups and anti-Austrian sentiment or encounter military action. Serbia called on Russia for support, and on July 28, Austria-Hungary declared war on Serbia. On August 1, Russian forces began mobilizing in support of Serbia, and Germany declared war on Russia. Russia's allies, Great Britain and France, then joined in.

ဆ

The **FIRST BATTLE OF THE MARNE** was the first significant battle that proved that the war would not be short, and introduced the fighting style most characteristic of World War I: trench warfare. By the end of August 1914, three of Germany's armies were moving toward Paris to take control of the city and conquer France. By September 3, half a million French civilians had left the city. The commander in chief of the French forces planned an attack on the

German First Army, and they attacked on September 6. By splitting the German armies, the French and the British were able to advance, and German forces couldn't break through. On September 9, the Germans retreated, and by September 10, the battle was over.

∽

The **BATTLE OF TANNENBERG** was fought from August 26 to August 31, 1914. It is considered Germany's greatest victory, and Russia's worst defeat. Two Russian armies, one led by General P.K. Rennenkampf, the other by A.V. Samsonov, planned on attacking East Prussia. Contact between the two armies was lost, and the Germans took advantage of Samsonov's isolated army. Within the next few days, half his army was lost, and on August 29, Samsonov shot himself. The Germans took 92,000 Russian prisoners.

∽

When the war broke out, the United States remained neutral and encouraged isolationism, even though there was pro-British propaganda spreading throughout the nation. On May 7, 1915, the RMS **LUSITA-NIA**, a British passenger ship that brought people to and from the United States and Britain, was sunk by a German U-boat. The sinking of the ship, with American citizens aboard, outraged the citizens of the United States. As wishes of neutrality started to wane, the British government intercepted the **ZIMMERMANN TELEGRAM**, which was sent to the German ambassador to Mexico instructing him to ask Mexico to attack the United States if the United States declared war on Germany. On April 6, 1917, the United States declared war on Germany.

∽

The Great War ended in 1918 with the **TREATY OF VERSAILLES**. The treaty was made by the British prime minister, the French prime minister, and President Woodrow Wilson. As a result of the treaty, much of the land Germany had acquired over the war was given back, the size of the German army and navy was dramatically reduced, and Germany would not be allowed to have an air force. Germany was forced to pay £6,600 million to compensate for damages, and the country had to take complete blame for the war. **THE LEAGUE OF NATIONS** was created in order to prevent any further conflicts.

THE GREAT DEPRESSION

Following World War I, America faced a time of economic expansion and the stock market became increasingly popular. Many saw the stock market as an easy way to get rich, and as stock prices rose, people viewed stocks as a safe way to invest. Stocks were being purchased on margin, meaning people who didn't have enough to pay for the stock would pay 10 to 20 percent up front and the broker would loan the rest. Not only did individuals put their money in the stock market, but companies and banks invested as well.

∽

On October 24, 1929 (Black Thursday), the New York Stock Exchange began to rapidly lose value and large numbers of people began selling their stocks. Five days later, Tuesday the 29th marked the worst day in the history of the stock market. Panic spread and people could not sell fast enough. With everyone selling and nobody buying, stocks plummeted and the market collapsed. That day, known as **BLACK TUESDAY**, more than 16.4 million shares of stock were sold, and the next day the stock market was closed. Black Tuesday is considered the beginning of the Great Depression.

∽

When **FRANKLIN DELANO ROOSEVELT** became president, he focused on reforming the nation and set forth the New Deal (a phrase coined during his nomination acceptance speech). The **NEW DEAL** was split into two phases. The first phase concentrated on regulating agriculture and business. During the first phase, programs like the National Recovery Administration, the Agricultural Adjustment Administration, and the Federal Communications Commission were established. The second phase focused more on relief for the working poor and social legislation. It was during the second phase that the Social Security Act was passed.

ᔕ

Though Roosevelt's New Deal reform helped, the **GREAT DEPRESSION** did not come to a complete end until the beginning of World War II. The numbers of the unemployed decreased by over 7 million in three years, and the number of people serving in the military increased by 8.6 million. While men fought overseas, women worked in the factories to produce weapons and materials for the war. Factories where vacuum cleaners had been made were now producing machine guns.

WORLD WAR II

On August 23, 1939, **HITLER** and **STALIN** agreed to the **NAZI-SOVIET PACT**. The invasion of Poland was originally set for August 26, but **MUSSOLINI** told Hitler that Italy was not yet ready for war, so the deadline was extended. On September 1, 1939, Adolf Hitler's Germany invaded and defeated Poland within weeks, in what was the first military engagement of World War II. Hitler believed this invasion would lead to a quick victory in this war. On September 3, Britain declared war on Germany.

ᔕ

Hitler wished to end the war swiftly, and knew an invasion of England was not the best way to go about it. Instead, he broke his pact with Stalin and invaded the Soviet Union. The German army invaded Russia on June 22, 1941, with a devastating blitzkrieg known as **OPERATION BARBAROSSA.** Within one week, 150,000 Soviet soldiers had been killed or wounded. The campaign lasted much longer than Hitler had anticipated, and the German armies could not withstand the Russian winter, giving the Soviets the advantage.

လ

The attack on the U.S. Naval base at **PEARL HARBOR** is what brought America into World War II. The Imperial Japanese Navy led a surprise attack at Pearl Harbor on December 7, 1941. The Japanese launched two attacks, sinking four U.S. battleships, killing 2,400 Americans, and wounding another 1,200. The next day, on December 8, the United States declared war on Japan. President Roosevelt famously announced to the American people, "Yesterday, December 7, 1941—**A DATE WHICH WILL LIVE IN INFAMY**—the United States was suddenly and deliberately attacked by naval and air forces of the Empire of Japan."

လ

By 1944, Germany knew the Allies would attempt to liberate Europe through an invasion of France. The Allied forces planned to land on the northwest coast of France, known as Normandy, under the code name Operation Overlord. On June 6, 1944, the Allies landed at five beaches on the **NORMANDY** coast. The Allied forces were met with heavy resistance from the defending Germans, but eventually they were able to make it through. The accomplishment of the Allied forces, and the failure of the Germans, put an end to Hitler's goal of a Nazi-controlled Europe.

လ

Germany's control and power began to weaken. As the Soviet Union fought German forces in the Battle of Berlin, Hitler, who had been hiding in a bunker during the battle, committed suicide. On May 1, the German forces surrendered in Italy, and on the next day, the forces fighting in Berlin surrendered to the Soviets. On May 7, the war in Europe was over. On August 6 and 9, the United States dropped two atomic bombs on Japan, and on August 14, Japan surrendered.

THE HOLOCAUST

In 1933, there were over 9 million Jews living in Europe. As Adolf Hitler came to power, he promoted hatred toward the Jewish people, believing Germans were a superior race and that Jews presented a threat to the community. The **HOLOCAUST** was Hitler's state-sponsored mass genocide of the Jewish people, in which approximately 6 million Jews were murdered. Jews were placed into ghettos, and then moved to concentration camps, and then extermination camps where they were gassed to death.

ᴕ

One way Adolf Hitler made the mass extermination of Jews possible was by eliciting strong feelings of ill will toward the Jewish community. He did so through propaganda in newspapers, film, art, music, books, radio, and the press. The weekly Nazi newspaper, *Der Stürmer*, meaning "The Attacker," featured caricatures of Jewish people as apelike. Films showed the Germans as superior, with an emphasis on German pride, and depicted the Jewish people as inferior, even subhuman. When Hitler came to power, he ruled with a combination of propaganda and a police state that silenced any critics.

ᴕ

From 1933 to 1939, the Jewish people were placed in **CONCENTRATION CAMPS**, where they were detained under horrible conditions. The first concentration camps began appearing as early as 1933 with

Hitler's appointment as chancellor. The very first concentration camp was at Dachau. Initially, these camps held political prisoners, but they would later go on to hold Jews, gays, gypsies, and those who were mentally ill, as well as anyone who opposed the regime. There were different types of concentration camps, and in 1939, forced labor camps began to appear. These required inmates to do physical labor under terrible conditions. Death was extremely common in these camps, but nothing would compare to the camps created to act out Hitler's "Final Solution."

In June of 1941, Germany began to enact the "**FINAL SOLUTION**." Mobile killing groups were created to gather up all of the Jews in towns, line them up, and shoot them one by one. By 1942, six death camps, or killing centers, were established near railway lines so that the Jewish people from concentration camps could be easily transported. The Jewish people, who at this point were forced to wear yellow stars on their clothing so they could be identified as Jews, were rounded up and taken to these death camps and gassed to death. Around 3.5 million Jewish people were killed in these camps. The largest of these camps was **AUSCHWITZ**.

As the Allies advanced through Germany, the concentration camps were gradually liberated. In total, an estimated 5 to 7 million Jewish people were killed as a result of the Holocaust. Around 50,000 to 100,000 remained in the Allies' zones of occupation, many refusing to ever go back to their homes, later being transported to the United States, Israel, and Palestine. **THE NUREMBERG TRIALS** began in October of 1945 and were presided over by American, British, French, and Russian judges. The first trial prosecuted twenty-one members of the Third Reich, including many of those responsible for the Holocaust.

THE COLD WAR

Following World War II, Europe was left completely devastated industrially, economically, and agriculturally, and the United States was the only major power that had not been left in ruins. In 1947, the **MARSHALL PLAN** was created by U.S. Secretary of State George Marshall to provide aid and restore political and economic stability to the Western countries. Marshall believed this plan could both rebuild the Western countries and blunt Communist advancement. A total of sixteen nations were involved in the program, and nearly $13 billion was distributed in financial aid.

∽

The **CUBAN MISSILE CRISIS** is considered the closest the United States ever came to a nuclear war. By the 1960s, the United States had missiles that could reach the Soviet Union, while the missiles of the Soviets could only reach as far as Europe. In 1962, the Soviets set their attention on Cuba and began putting their intermediate-range missiles there. Photographs of the Soviet missiles in Cuba surfaced, and a naval quarantine was deployed around Cuba. Tension grew as communication between the United States and the Soviet Union continued. Finally, the Soviet Union agreed to dismantle the installations in hopes that the United States would not invade Cuba.

∽

On October 4, 1957, the Soviets launched the first artificial satellite into space, *SPUTNIK 1*. The launch was a surprise to Americans, who believed they were the leaders in technology, and many feared *Sputnik* was a weapon. The United States launched the **EXPLORER 1** only four months after *Sputnik*. The Soviet Union originally led in the **SPACE RACE**. In April of 1961, the Soviet Union was the first to launch a man into orbit (twenty-three days later, the United States sent their first man into orbit), and in June of 1963, the Soviet Union sent the very first woman into orbit. Ultimately, the United States won the Space Race. In 1961, President Kennedy announced the goal of sending a man to the Moon, and eight years later, that goal was achieved.

EXTRACURRICULARS: YEARBOOK
MOST LIKELY TO TAKE ONE GIANT LEAP FOR MANKIND

On July 20, 1969, the entire world watched as the Apollo 11 crew landed and Neil Armstrong and "Buzz" Aldrin became the first two men to ever walk on the Moon. Armstrong's immortal words were broadcast as he took his first steps: "One small step for [a] man, one giant leap for mankind."

The **BERLIN WALL** was more than just a division between West and East Germany. It was symbolic of democracy versus communism. The split had also occurred in the capital, Berlin. West Berlin was actually encircled by the rest of East Germany. While West Germany experienced economic growth, East Germany, under the Soviet Union's communist influence, had a dragging economy and individual rights were severely restricted. By the 1950s, many residents of East Germany were fleeing to West Berlin. Once there, they were able to fly to West Germany. By 1961, 2.5 million people had left East Germany, and several attempts, with the help of the Soviet Union, were made to control West Berlin, until finally a wall was built that stretched hundreds of miles. The Berlin Wall was torn down in 1989.

In 1985, **MIKHAIL GORBACHEV** became president of the Soviet Union, and as desperately needed reform was being promoted in the country Gorbachev introduced **PERESTROIKA**, a restructuring of the economy, and **GLASNOST**, which allowed for political freedom. As reforms continued throughout 1986–1990, Soviet states gained new autonomy, and Gorbachev's power and ability to hold the Union together weakened. In 1991, a coup was attempted against Gorbachev. The coup failed, but Gorbachev lost support and Boris Yeltsin came to power. The USSR was dissolved and the **RUSSIAN FEDERATION** was created.

9/11 AND THE WAR ON TERROR

On **SEPTEMBER 11, 2001**, four commercial passenger jet airliners were hijacked by nineteen **AL-QAEDA** terrorists. Two of the planes crashed into the twin towers of the **WORLD TRADE CENTER** in New York City. Within two hours, both of the towers collapsed, killing 2,752 people, including 343 firefighters, and 60 police officers. The third plane crashed into the Pentagon, killing 184 people. After hearing about the other two attacks, the passengers and crew aboard the fourth hijacked flight attempted to retake the plane, and the plane crashed near Shanksville, Pennsylvania, killing all 44 people on board. In 2004, **OSAMA BIN LADEN** claimed responsibility for the attacks.

⌀

Following the attacks of September 11, the Bush administration declared the **WAR ON TERROR**. The objectives of the war were to defeat terrorists and their organizations (including Osama bin Laden and Abu Musab al-Zarqawi), strengthen the international effort to combat terrorism, deny any forms of support or sanctuary to terrorist organizations, reduce conditions that terrorists can exploit, and defend U.S. interests at home and abroad.

⌀

On October 7, 2001, the **WAR IN AFGHANISTAN** began with the launch of **OPERATION ENDURING FREEDOM**. The goal of

Operation Enduring Freedom was to dismantle the al-Qaeda organization, end its use of Afghanistan as its base, remove the Taliban, and locate Osama bin Laden. The first phase of Operation Enduring Freedom saw the Taliban thrown out of power in Kabul. In 2002, Operation Anaconda was launched to destroy any al-Qaeda and Taliban that remained. The Taliban came together in Pakistan and unleashed offensives on the coalition forces.

ဢ

In March 2003, the **WAR IN IRAQ** began. First, Iraq was attacked from the air, and then ground forces went in. Though the reasons for the war have been questioned, the Bush administration claimed that it was part of the war against terrorism and that Iraq housed terrorists and weapons of mass destruction. In April 2003, Baghdad fell and the government of **SADDAM HUSSEIN** dissolved soon after. President Bush announced the war was over; however, an insurgency occurred that actually led to more casualties than the initial invasion. No weapons of mass destruction were found. In December 2003, Saddam Hussein was captured, and in 2006, he was hanged. U.S. combat ended on September 1, 2010, with Operation New Dawn.

ဢ

On May 2, 2011, ten years after the attacks of September 11, **OSAMA BIN LADEN** was killed. The operation was called **OPERATION NEP-TUNE SPEAR**, and was ordered by President Barack Obama. A team of U.S. Navy SEALs from the United States Naval Special Warfare Development Group (or SEAL Team Six) raided the compound in Pakistan where bin Laden had been living. Following the raid, bin Laden's body was taken to Afghanistan to be identified and then was buried at sea following Muslim practices. On May 6, his death was confirmed by al-Qaeda.

PERIOD 5
PHYS. ED.

FOR THIS CLASS, you don't have to try to fit into your old gym uniform, do fifty pull-ups, or even get creamed in a game of dodge ball. When you were in school, the point of your physical education class, believe it or not, was not humiliation, but to give you a little exercise during the day and to teach you that discipline and friendly competition will help you succeed in life. Now let's see that discipline put to work to learn some facts you may have forgotten about sports.

FRESHMAN YEAR: TRACK AND FIELD & SWIMMING

TRACK AND FIELD

TRACK AND FIELD refers to various athletic contests including running, jumping, and throwing, typically performed inside a stadium with a grass field enclosed by a track.

ɯɔ

The first recorded track and field events occurred at the ancient **OLYMPIC GAMES**. The earliest known games were played in 776 B.C.E. and consisted of only a 192m race.

ɯɔ

The ancient Olympic pentathlon included the long jump, javelin throw, discus throw, a footrace, and wresting.

ɯɔ

The track and field running events include sprints (60m, 100m, 200m, 400m), middle distance (800m, 1500m, 3000m), long-distance (5,000m, 10,000m), hurdles, and relays.

ɯɔ

The jumping and throwing events include the long jump, high jump, pole vault, shot put, discus throw, hammer throw, and javelin throw.

ɯɔ

Combined events include the modern pentathlon, heptathlon, and decathlon.

Tug of war was once a track and field game at the Olympics, but has not been played since 1920.

EXTRACURRICULARS: NEWSPAPER
JIM THORPE STRIPPED OF MEDALS

At the 1912 Summer Olympics in Stockholm, **JIM THORPE** won the gold in both the pentathlon and decathlon, but a year later, his medals were stripped by the International Olympic Committee. At the time, there were strict rules that athletes must be amateurs to compete, but it was discovered that Thorpe had played professional baseball before training for Sweden. In 1982, thirty years after his death, the medals were reinstated after lobbying from Thorpe's supporters.

FLORENCE GRIFFITH JOYNER (or Flo-Jo) holds the world record for the women's 100m dash (10.49 seconds), and 200m dash (21.34 seconds).

The **MARATHON** was added to the Olympics in 1921. The official distance is 26.22 miles.

The fastest marathon world records are 2:03:23 for men, held by Wilson Kipsang Kiprotich of Kenya; and 2:15:25 for women held by Paula Radcliffe of Great Britain.

MARION JONES was stripped of three track and field gold medals won during the 2000 Summer Olympics after admitting to doping.

USAIN BOLT, a Jamaican sprinter who holds the world record for both the 100m and 200m dash, is the highest paid track and field athlete of all time.

SWIMMING

SWIMMING was introduced at the first modern Olympic Games in Athens in 1896. Women were first allowed to swim in the Olympics in 1912.

In 1956, the **BUTTERFLY STROKE** became a separate competition. From 1933 until then, it was a variation used by swimmers in the breaststroke competition.

THERE ARE FOUR STROKES IN COMPETITIVE SWIMMING:

1. Front crawl (or freestyle)
2. Backstroke
3. Breaststroke
4. Butterfly

MEDLEY SWIMMING is when all four strokes are performed.

An **OLYMPIC-SIZE SWIMMING POOL** is required to be 25 meters by 50 meters (or about 82 feet by 164 feet).

Olympic-size pools have a regulation ten lanes, and are used for what is referred to as the "long course."

In 1984, Olympic swimming had its first tie. U.S. swimmers Carrie Steinseifer and Nancy Hogshead-Makar completed the 100m freestyle competition touching the wall at a time of 55.92 seconds.

MICHAEL PHELPS is an American swimmer who has won sixteen gold medals, broken five records in one meet, and has won more Olympic medals than anyone else in the history of the Olympics, with a total of twenty-two medals.

DARA TORRES is an American swimmer who was the first to compete in five Olympic Games. In the 2008 Beijing Olympics, Torres competed at the age of forty-one, making her the oldest American swimmer in Olympic history.

GERTRUDE EDERLE was the first woman to swim the English Channel (about 21 miles) in 1926.

The first outdoor swimming pool was added to the White House by Gerald Ford in 1976.

SOPHOMORE YEAR: SOCCER & TENNIS

SOCCER

SOCCER is one of the oldest sports in the world. No one is quite sure when or where it started. China was the first country to actually write about a game that involved kicking a round object into a goal, and that game was played more than 4,000 years ago. The game was called tsu chu, and it was played for the emperor's birthday.

∽

In 1848, Cambridge University first attempted to standardize a set of rules for the game of football (or soccer in the United States) but no one could fully agree.

∽

It wasn't until October 26, 1863, that the **FOOTBALL ASSOCIATION** formed in London and established the official rules to the game.

∽

On May 21, 1904, the **FÉDÉRATION INTERNATIONALE DE FOOT-BALL ASSOCIATION (FIFA)** was established.

∽

Soccer became an Olympic sport in 1904.

∽

THE WORLD CUP is a soccer tournament held every four years to determine a world champion.

ꜱ

BRAZIL has won the most World Cup championships, with five wins. **ITALY** and **GERMANY** have each won the World Cup four times.

ꜱ

SOME KEY TERMS:

- **GIVE-AND-GO:** A way of getting around a defender by bouncing the ball off one of your teammates.
- **HEADER:** When a player uses his head to direct the ball.
- **PENALTY BOX:** The area in front of the goal inside the 18-yard line.

ꜱ

PELÉ is considered one of the greatest players of all time. He played in four World Cup Championships with Brazil, and is the top career scorer of all time.

ꜱ

DIEGO MARADONA is also considered one of the greatest players in soccer, having played in four World Cups for Argentina. He is most known for the "hand of God" from the 1986 World Cup, in which he scored with a handball that wasn't penalized because the referee didn't see it.

TENNIS

Monks in the twelfth century began playing a game very similar to **TENNIS**, but used their hands instead of a racket.

ꜱ

In London, 1874, the rules for a game similar to today's tennis were laid out.

The first **WIMBLEDON** tournament was held in 1877, and by 1882, the rules for modern tennis were established.

Tennis tournaments are generally divided by gender, number of players (singles or doubles), and mixed doubles (one male, one female).

There are four main tournaments:

1. **THE AUSTRALIAN OPEN**—played on hard courts
2. **THE FRENCH OPEN**—played on clay
3. **WIMBLEDON**—played on grass
4. **THE U.S. OPEN**—played on hard courts

Having a **GRAND SLAM** means winning all four tournaments in the same year.

SOME KEY TERMS:

- **FAULT:** A service not in play.
- **LOVE:** Zero points in a match.
- **SET POINT:** The final point needed by a player for the win.

SOME IMPORTANT PLAYERS:

- **SERENA WILLIAMS** has won eighteen Grand Slam singles titles. Her sister, **VENUS WILLIAMS**, has won seven.

- **RAPHAEL NADAL** has won five Grand Slam singles titles and also took home the gold medal from the 2008 Beijing Olympics.
- **ROD LAVER** won the Grand Slam twice in his career, one time in 1962, and the other in 1969.

EXTRACURRICULARS: YEARBOOK
MOST LIKELY TO NEED MORE SPACE IN THE TROPHY CASE

Tennis star **STEFFI GRAF** holds the record for most Grand Slam tournament wins. She won 22.

JUNIOR YEAR: BASKETBALL & HOCKEY

BASKETBALL

In 1891, Dr. James Naismith invented **BASKETBALL** at a YMCA in Springfield, Massachusetts, as a way to keep students occupied during the winter. It was called basket ball (then two words) because students would throw a ball into peach baskets.

∽

Nine of the original thirteen rules have been modified and are still used in basketball today.

∽

There are currently thirty teams in the **NATIONAL BASKETBALL ASSOCIATION** (NBA).

In the playoffs, teams from the Eastern Conference and the Western Conference play against each other in a best-of-seven tournament. The final four teams play against each other in the NBA Conference Finals.

SOME FAMOUS PLAYERS:

- **LARRY BIRD:** Player for the Boston Celtics. He was Most Valuable Player (MVP) three times, won the championship three times and an Olympic Gold Medal, and had a rivalry with Magic Johnson that was legendary.
- **MICHAEL JORDAN:** Player for the Chicago Bulls. He was MVP seven times and led the Bulls to six championships.
- **WILT CHAMBERLAIN:** Thought by many to be one of the greatest basketball players in history, Chamberlain was MVP four times, and won one championship with the Philadelphia 76ers and one with the Los Angeles Lakers. Before playing in the NBA, Chamberlain played for the Harlem Globetrotters.

The Boston Celtics have won the most NBA championships.

EXTRACURRICULARS: STUDENT COUNCIL

BILL BRADLEY played for ten years on the New York Knicks before successfully running as a New Jersey senator in 1978. He retired in 1997, and tried to run for president in 2000, but did not win a single primary.

Basketball and hockey are the only two major sports in which every team faces off with one another.

HOCKEY

Though its origins are unknown, the first **HOCKEY** game played with established rules was in 1875 in Montreal, Canada, by students of McGill University.

The **NATIONAL HOCKEY LEAGUE (NHL)** was established in 1917.

In 1920, ice hockey was played in the Summer Olympics in Belgium for the first time.

The NHL is divided into two conferences: Eastern and Western, which are then divided into three divisions.

In a regular season, eighty-two games are played and teams are given points:

- If a team wins, it's two points.
- If a team ties, it's one point.
- If a team loses in overtime, it's one point.
- If a team loses, it's zero points.

The eight teams from each conference with the most points face off in the playoffs, which are made up of four rounds. The two winners from these rounds face off in the **STANLEY CUP**, where they play best-of-seven.

The two winners

Hockey is one of the few sports where violence is encouraged, but penalties are enforced. While checking or smashing into players is allowed, boarding or smashing the other player into the boards is penalized.

The Montreal Canadiens have won more Stanley Cup championships than any other team, with twenty-three wins, and one win before the formation of the NHL.

SOME FAMOUS PLAYERS:

- **WAYNE GRETZKY:** Nicknamed "the Great One," he played for twenty seasons, and still holds sixty NHL records.
- **HENRIK SEDIN:** Captain for the Vancouver Canucks. In the 2009–2010 season, Sedin won the Hart Memorial Trophy and was deemed MVP.
- **SIDNEY CROSBY:** Captain for the Pittsburgh Penguins. In 2009, Crosby became the youngest captain to win the Stanley Cup in NHL history.
- **BOBBY HULL:** Recorded the fastest slap shot of all time at 118.3 mph.
- **MANON RHÉAUME:** Played goalie during two exhibition games for the Tampa Bay Lightning, making her the only woman to ever play in the NHL.
- **GORDIE HOWE:** Holds the record for most career games with 1,767.

SENIOR YEAR: BASEBALL & FOOTBALL

BASEBALL

The first mention of the game of **BASEBALL** was in a British publication in 1744.

ഗ

In 1845, Alexander Cartwright created the Knickerbocker Rules, a code that detailed how to play baseball. Many of these rules are still in place today.

ഗ

The **WORLD SERIES** is the championship between the two best teams of the season. The first team to win four out of seven games is the winner of the series.

ഗ

With twenty-seven wins, the New York Yankees have won the World Series more than any other team.

ഗ

SOME KEY TERMS:

- **CLUTCH HITTER:** A high honor for a player, the clutch hitter is able to hit the ball when it matters the most and the game is on the line.
- **GOLDEN SOMBRERO:** When a player strikes out four times in a game.

- **HIT AND RUN:** When a runner on first base makes a break for second as the pitch is thrown. If the batter does not hit the ball, the runner will be stealing the base and will be counted out.
- **RUNS BATTED IN (RBI):** The number of runs scored as a direct result of the person at bat.

ᴄᴏ

SOME FAMOUS PLAYERS:

- **BABE RUTH:** Also known as the Sultan of Swat, when Babe Ruth retired in 1935, he held the record for most home runs with 714. His record was not beaten until 1974 by **HANK AARON**.
- **JACKIE ROBINSON:** First black player to enter the major leagues in 1947, he contributed greatly to ending segregation in baseball.
- **JOE DIMAGGIO:** Played all thirteen years of his career with the Yankees and is best known for a fifty-six-game hitting streak, a record that still stands today.

ᴄᴏ

In 1919, the **CHICAGO WHITE SOX** played in the World Series against the Cincinnati Reds. The first baseman and six other players teamed up with a group of gamblers and decided to throw the games. Shortly after losing all five games, their plans were discovered and all the players involved were banned from baseball permanently.

ᴄᴏ

PETE ROSE was Rookie of the Year in 1963, MVP in 1973, and won three World Series. When he was manager of the Cincinnati Reds, reports spread that Rose was gambling on his team. In 1987, Rose was banned from baseball. In 2007, Pete Rose finally admitted that he bet on his team "every night."

In 2002, the issue of **STEROID USE** in baseball came to a head. In 2004, José Canseco released an autobiography claiming that 80 percent of all players used steroids. Steroid use had become so widespread that Congress stepped in, which led to new testing rules and disciplines.

FOOTBALL

The roots of **FOOTBALL** trace back to both rugby and soccer.

In 1876, **WALTER CAMP**, considered to be the father of football, created the first rules for American football, and in the early twentieth century football spread across college campuses. The **NATIONAL FOOTBALL LEAGUE** (NFL) was established in 1920. Originally it was called the American Professional Football Association.

There are no playoffs in college football. Instead teams play **BOWL GAMES** among their divisions. The oldest and most prestigious are the Rose Bowl, the Orange Bowl, and the Sugar Bowl.

The **HEISMAN TROPHY** is given each year to the most outstanding college player.

Currently, there are thirty-two teams in the NFL, divided into two conferences: the National Football Conference (NFC) and the American Football Conference (AFC).

During the NFL playoffs, six teams from each conference play against one another. The two winning teams play against each other in the **SUPER BOWL**.

The Pittsburgh Steelers have won the Super Bowl six times. The San Francisco 49ers and the Dallas Cowboys have each won five times.

SOME FOOTBALL FACTS:

- **EMMITT SMITH** holds the record for the **MOST NFL RUSHING YARDS** with 18,355.
- **JERRY RICE** has scored more **TOUCHDOWNS** than any other player with 208.
- The **UNIVERSITY OF ALABAMA** has won fourteen college National Championships, more than any other school.
- **BO JACKSON**, **REGGIE BUSH**, **TIM TEBOW**, **JOHNNY MAN-ZIEL**, and **JAMEIS WINSTON** are all Heisman Trophy winners.

EXTRACURRICULARS: DRAMA CLUB

Earning more than $300 million at the global box office, *The Blind Side* is the highest-grossing sports film of all time. It tells the real life story of NFL player Michael Oher and his adoptive parents.

PERIOD 6
MATHEMATICS

YOU MAY NOT REMEMBER the Fibonacci numbers or the Pythagorean theorem off the top of your head, but learning the fundamentals of algebra, geometry, trigonometry, and calculus back in high school prepared you for the problem-solving you have to do every day in your life. It probably doesn't seem like it, but you use math daily, whether it's getting to work on time, paying your bills, or calculating when a train that left Dallas at 9 A.M. will meet a train that left Chicago at 10:30 A.M. Okay, so maybe not that last one, but this course in mathematics will give you a good refresher on everything you used to know about x and y.

FRESHMAN YEAR: ALGEBRA

ALGEBRA TERMS

ALGEBRA is a branch of mathematics that uses symbols to represent quantities and involves methods for solving equations that contain unknown variables. "Classical algebra"—the process of solving equations—has developed over 4,000 years, while "abstract algebra"—the study of groups, rings, and fields—has appeared in the last 200 years.

∽

ADDITION is literally the process of adding, or combining, one thing to another thing. So in the problem 3 + 6, you are adding or combining the two numbers together, giving you an end result of 9.

∽

SUBTRACTION, the inverse of addition, means to take a certain number away from the original value. So for example, if you subtract 3 from 10 (expressed as 10 − 3), you are left with 7.

∽

MULTIPLICATION is the process of repeated addition. For example, 5 × 4 is simply saying 5 added to itself 4 times, or 5 + 5 + 5 + 5. There are many ways to represent multiplication. The first and most common is by using the multiplication sign ×. Multiplication can also be expressed as a dot, such as 5 • 4, or by placing numbers side by side with parentheses between them, such as 5(4).

DIVISION is the opposite of multiplication. It is the process of splitting something into equal parts. Division can be represented in several ways. The most common symbol is ÷, but it can also be expressed with / between two numbers or with a bar between two numbers like in a fraction. So, if 5 × 4 = 20, then 20 ÷ 5 = 4. The problem can also be expressed as 20/5 or $\frac{20}{5}$.

DECIMALS are another way of expressing a fraction. The fraction ⅘ is equivalent to 0.8. Each number after the decimal is based on the number 10. Therefore, 0.8 is actually eight tenths. A number in the next spot to the right would make it hundredths, and the next spot to the right would make it thousandths. For example, 0.54 is the same as saying fifty-four hundredths, and 0.986 is the same as saying nine-hundred eighty-six thousandths.

Finding the **PERCENT** of a number is very easy. If you are asked, "What percent of 98 is 32?" you must first divide 32 by 98. The answer is 0.32653061. Choose the first four numbers, and remember to round. You now have 0.3265. Then multiply this number by 100, leaving you with 32.65, and then round to the nearest whole number. So, 32 is 33 percent of 98.

SQUARING A NUMBER is multiplying that number by itself. It is represented by a superscript 2 (the exponent) next to the number that you are going to multiply. So, 4^2 is equal to 16, because 4 × 4 = 16. The **SQUARE ROOT** is the inverse of squaring and is represented by the symbol √. **PERFECT SQUARES** are squares of whole numbers. For example, $\sqrt{100} = 10$ because $10^2 = 100$, and that is perfect square, a whole number. However, $\sqrt{105} = 10.246951$, and that is not a whole number, and therefore, not a perfect square.

∽

A **FACTORIAL** is a very simple concept to understand. It is expressed by an exclamation point following a number (for example, 5!). Factorials are the product (meaning result from multiplication) of all of the positive integers less than or equal to that number. So, 5! is really saying $5 \times 4 \times 3 \times 2 \times 1 = 120$.

ALGEBRAIC EXPRESSIONS

An example of a single **ALGEBRAIC EXPRESSION** is $6x$, where 6 represents the **COEFFICIENT** and x represents the **VARIABLE**, and these numbers are multiplied together. You can only add and subtract like terms. For example, in $7x + 9z$, x and z are unlike terms and the problem thus cannot be simplified further; however, with $7x + 9x$, the variables are both x, and you can work the problem out to $16x$.

∽

With multiplication it is a matter of following the laws regarding **EXPONENTS**. For example:

$$x^4(x^3 + 6a) = x^7 + 6ax^4$$

That is the simplest answer you can get from this problem. With problems that have two sets of equations in parentheses, break up the first set and distribute across both equations:

$$(x + 7)\,(a - 2)$$

$$x(a - 2) + 7(a - 2)$$

Add or subtract the problems based on whether the second part of the problem is positive or negative. So that gives us:

$$xa - 2x + 7a - 14$$

You cannot break it down further, so that is our answer.

∽

When dividing algebraic expressions, first write out the problem as a fraction. The next step is to simplify the coefficient, and then cancel out like variables in both the numerator and the denominator. For example:

$$8ab^4 \div 2ab = \frac{8 \times a \times b \times b \times b \times b}{2 \times a \times b} = 4b^3$$

∽

When solving for x, you want to get x all by itself. For example:

$$2x = 10$$

To get x by itself, you have to divide $2x$ by 2, and whatever you do on one side, you must do on the other side. So you end up with $x = 5$. No matter how complex the problem might get, as long as you remember to get x by itself, you will be able to solve the problem.

∽

Rearranging formulas is essentially taking all that you have learned and working backward. It is very similar to the last lesson where you solved for x, only you are not limited to just one number. You can solve any part of the problem. For example, if you have a formula that states $2b = c$, and you are asked to solve for b, you can divide both sides by 2. So, b = $c/2$.

LINEAR EQUATIONS

A **LINEAR EQUATION** is an algebraic equation that features a constant (or product of a constant) and a single variable that is only the first power. For example, $x + 6$, $4x + 7y$, and $5x + 3$ are all linear equations. However x^2 is not, because x^2 is not the first power; $4xy + 6$ is not because more than one variable is multiplied; and $6x/8y$ is not because you cannot divide two different variables.

∽

FUNCTIONS are essential to mathematic equations, and even though you might not know what they are called, you have already seen and worked with examples of functions. For example, $7x + 3 = y$. To find y, you need to find x. When y depends on finding x, and only one possible answer can be found, that is a function. No matter what x equals, there can only be one value for y.

∽

POLYNOMIALS are expressions that are the sum of exponents and variables. Each section of the polynomial is considered a term. To be considered a polynomial, terms must follow strict rules. There cannot be any square roots of variables, fractions, or fractional powers. There must be variables that are raised to a whole number exponent or a regular number. A polynomial looks like this:

$$7x^2 + 8x - 9$$

And do not be fooled by the $8x$. It still follows the rules of terms because it is the same as saying $8x^1$.

QUADRATICS

Polynomials that follow the pattern $ax^2 + bx + c$ have a special name. They are called **QUADRATICS**. To factor quadratics, you need to find numbers that when multiplied equal c, but when added equal b. For example:

$$x2 + 6x + 8$$

You first break it down into two sets to multiply:

$$(x + ?)\,(x + ?)$$

Then plug in numbers and test:

$$(x + 4)\,(x + 2) = x^2 + 2x + 4x + 8 = x^2 + 6x + 8$$

Therefore, your answer is $(x + 4)\,(x + 2)$.

∽

Some quadratic equations cannot be factored. To solve these, a method called **COMPLETING THE SQUARE** is used. This turns $ax^2 + bx + c$ into $ax^2 + bx + c = (a + b)^2$. For example:

$$x^2 + 2x + 1 = 0$$

Begin by transposing the constant term:

$$x^2 + 2x = -1$$

Then add a square to both sides. To do so, take half of the coefficient of x and then square it. So, half of 2 is 1, and then 1^2 is 1.

$$x^2 + 2x + 1 = -1 + 1$$

$$x^2 + 2x + 1 = 0$$

Now you have $(x + 1)\,(x + 1) = 0$.

Break these up into two individual problems:

$$x + 1 = 0 \text{ and } x + 1 = 0$$

Solve for x. In both cases, x equals -1. Your answer will go in brackets and look like this:

$$\{-1, -1\}$$

ↇ

Another way to solve a quadratic equation is to use the **QUADRATIC FORMULA**. Each solution produced by the formula provides a root. The formula states:

$$x = \frac{-b \pm \sqrt{b^2 - 4ac}}{2a}$$

ↇ

A **COMPLEX NUMBER** is a number that consists of two parts: a real part and an imaginary part. Complex numbers allow problems that would not otherwise be solved with real numbers to be solved. The imaginary number is introduced by using the letter i, and is based on the formula $a + bi$. The letters a and b represent real numbers and i equals the square root of -1.

ↇ

When graphing algebraic functions, we use the Cartesian coordinate system, where each point on the graph is represented by an x coordinate and a y coordinate. For example, if you were to graph $y = x$, the coordinates would include (0,0), (1,1), (2,2), (-1,-1), (-2,-2), to infinity.

ↇ

The graph of a linear equation is a straight light. The graph of a quadratic equation is a parabola. Each point that crosses the horizontal axis (when $y = 0$) is a root.

Graphing functions provided the first major historic link between algebra and geometry.

EXTRACURRICULARS: YEARBOOK
MOST LIKELY TO BE INFINITE

One of the greatest mathematicians of all time, **EUCLID** added much to the mathematical cannon, but he is perhaps best known for the proof that there are infinitely many prime numbers, numbers that are only divisible by themselves and 1. He discovered this through a proof by contradiction.

SOPHOMORE YEAR: GEOMETRY

GEOMETRY TERMS

GEOMETRY is a branch of mathematics that considers the shapes of objects, spatial relationships, and the properties of surrounding space. Its name is derived from two Greek words for *ge*, meaning "earth," and *metron*, meaning "measurement." The Egyptians used geometry to build the pyramids and survey fields; they were able to measure lines and angles and calculate areas and volumes.

ᴪ

POLYGONS are particular types of shapes used in geometry. Polygons have many straight sides. With regular polygons, all of the **ANGLES** and **SIDES** have to be the same. A shape with three sides and angles is called a **TRIANGLE**. A shape with four sides and angles is called a **QUADRILATERAL**. A shape with five sides and angles is a **PENTAGON**, six makes a **HEXAGON**, and so on. A shape that has two pairs of parallel lines is called a **PARALLELOGRAM**.

ဟ

PERIMETER is a very simple idea, with a very simple solution to finding it. The perimeter of an object is the distance around the outside of the shape. The easiest way of finding the perimeter is by adding up the length of all of the sides. For example, if a rectangle has two sides that are 7 inches and two sides that are 3 inches, then the perimeter would be 7 + 7 + 3 + 3 = 20.

ဟ

The **AREA** is the amount of space inside a shape. To find the area of a square or any other plane shape, the formula is simple. You multiply the length by the height of the object. To find the area of a parallelogram, you multiply the base by the height of the object. For trapezoids—shapes with four sides but only one pair of parallel sides—you add the lengths of the two parallel sides, divide by two, and then multiply that number by the height.

ဟ

CIRCUMFERENCE is the same idea as perimeter, only it applies to circles. The formula to find the circumference requires a little more work, however. To find the circumference, multiply the diameter of the circle by π, which as you may recall, is simplified to 3.14. If only the radius is provided, multiply the radius by 2 to find the diameter, and then solve for the circumference.

ဟ

Whereas area deals with two-dimensional figures, **VOLUME** is the amount of space in three-dimensional figures. To find the volume of a rectangular prism, multiply the length by the width by the height. To find the volume of a triangular prism, complete the same formula and then multiply by ½. As the shapes get more advanced, so too do the formulas for volume. For example, the formula for finding the volume of a cone is ⅓ times the area of the base times the height.

☙

The **SURFACE AREA** of a shape is the sum of all of the areas. For rectangular prisms, finding the surface area requires finding the area of each side and adding them together. This can be simplified by finding the area of one side and then multiplying it by two (because there are two sides), and then doing the same thing for the other side. To find the surface area of a cylinder, the formula is $2\pi r^2 + 2\pi rh$

ANGLES

An **ANGLE** is formed when two rays, an order of points in a line, share the same endpoint. The size of an angle refers to the value of the arc between the two lines, or the value of the rotation.

☙

As angles increase, their names change. **ACUTE** angles have values that are greater than zero but less than 90 degrees. A **RIGHT** angle is exactly 90 degrees. An **OBTUSE** angle is any angle greater than 90 degrees but less than 180 degrees. A **REFLEX** angle is larger than an obtuse angle, and it is any angle that is more than 180 but less than 360. A **PERIGON** is a full rotation that equals 360 degrees exactly.

☙

COMPLEMENTARY angles are any two angles that when added together equal 90 degrees. This means that if you put them together, they will form a right angle.

A **SUPPLEMENTARY** angle is the sum of any two angles that equals 180 degrees. This means that when they are added together, they make a straight line.

∽

The angle is defined by the **THETA SYMBOL, Θ**. The length of the arc is represented by the lowercase letter s, and the radius of a circle is represented by the lowercase letter r. The lowercase letter k is used to represent a scaling constant, and depends on the units of measurement in the problem. The basic formula for finding the value of an angle is:

$$\theta = k\,\frac{s}{r}$$

∽

If an angle is counterclockwise, the angle (θ) will have a **POSITIVE** value. If the angle is in a clockwise motion, then the value of θ will be **NEGATIVE**. θ equaling -50° and θ equaling 50° do not mean the same thing. Angles have degrees of rotation and directions of rotation. Even though both of those numbers have the same degree of rotation, their directions are the opposite, making them different angles.

THE PYTHAGOREAN THEOREM

The **PYTHAGOREAN THEOREM** is one of the best-known formulas ever written:

$$a^2 + b^2 = c^2$$

The letters a and b represent the sides of the triangle, and the letter c represents the hypotenuse, which is opposite of the right angle.

The Pythagorean theorem can only be used when dealing with right triangles (which as you might recall, means an angle of 90 degrees). There are at least 370 ways to prove the Pythagorean theorem.

∽

The **PYTHAGOREAN TRIPLE** is a series of three whole numbers, such as 3, 4, and 5 that work when put into the Pythagorean theorem, and can be the sides of a right triangle. Other examples of Pythagorean triples include 5, 12, 13 and 7, 24, 25. To create a Pythagorean triple, take any odd number and square it. Then find two consecutive numbers that add up to that number.

CURVES

A **CURVE** is similar to a line in that it is a continuously moving point, but it does not have to be straight. A curve starts out like a straight line then begins to deform in a smooth and continuous formation. The shape of the curve is the result of a particular equation. Closed curves repeat and open curves have infinite length.

∽

The most common curve is the **CIRCLE**. The circle is made up of a determinate line. It does not extend forever, but rather has an end point. When drawing curves on a graph with an x and y axis, a basic formula that tells you the curve will be a circle is $x^2 + y^2 = a^2$. Both values are squared, making them positive, and both have the same coefficient, making them equal distances. Another formula for making a circle is:

$$(x - h)^2 + (y - k)^2 = r^2$$

In this formula, h and k represent the x and y coordinates that are found in the center of the circle, and r is the radius. For example, if

you have coordinates (8, 5) with a radius of 10, your circle would be
$(x - 8)^2 + (y - 5)^2 = 100$.

∽

An ellipse resembles a circle, only it is squashed and is oval. Ellipses
are defined by two points, known as foci (F_1) and (F_2). At any point
of the ellipse, if the distances of the focus points are added up, they
are constant. The basic formula for an ellipse is:

$$\frac{(x - h)^2}{a^2} + \frac{(y - k)^2}{b^2} = 1$$

∽

A **PARABOLA** is a curve that is U-shaped. It is the locus of a point
that is always the same distance from the focus and a given line,
called the directrix. The standard equations for making parabolas
are:

$$y - k = a(x - h)^2 \quad \text{and} \quad x - h = a(y - k)^2$$

If a is greater than zero, the parabola opens upward, and if it is less
than zero, it opens downward.

∽

A **HYPERBOLA** is kind of like two parabolas put together, making
a sort of X shape. There are two types of hyperbolas: vertical and
horizontal. The formula for a vertical hyperbola is:

$$\frac{(y - v)^2}{a^2} + \frac{(x - h)^2}{b^2} = 1$$

The formula for a horizontal hyperbola is:

$$\frac{(x - h)^2}{a^2} + \frac{(y - v)^2}{b^2} = 1$$

§

PI is a **MATHEMATICAL CONSTANT**. Pi is always equal to the ratio between the area of a circle, and its radius squared. Pi is represented by the Greek letter π. The symbol name is pi, and it is the symbol still used today.

§

To put it simply, π expresses the ratio of a circle's circumference to its diameter. Regardless of the size of the circle, this ratio will always equal π.

§

Pi is an **IRRATIONAL CONSTANT**, which means that it cannot be expressed as a fraction or ratio of two integers. Pi is also a **TRANSCENDENTAL NUMBER**, meaning that it is not the root of any algebraic number. When pi is calculated out into numbers, the decimal representation does not repeat or end. For example, the number truncated to 50 decimals is 3.14159265358979323846264338327950288 419716939937510. So for basic mathematic equations, many people shorten pi to 3.14.

EXTRACURRICULARS: NEWSPAPER
DR. MARYAM MIRZAKHANI BECOMES FIRST WOMAN TO WIN FIELDS MEDAL

In 2014, Stanford University mathematician **DR. MARYAM MIR-ZAKHANI** won the Fields Medal, the most prestigious award in mathematics for her work on the understanding of the symmetry of curved surfaces. She is the first woman to ever win the prize.

JUNIOR YEAR: TRIGONOMETRY AND PRE-CALCULUS

TRIGONOMETRIC FUNCTIONS

TRIGONOMETRY literally means "measurement of triangles," and that is exactly what it is: the study of triangles.

∽

Trigonometric functions, which describe the ratios between sides of **RIGHT TRIANGLES**, include: sine (sin), cosine (cos), tangent (tan), cotangent (cot), secant (sec), and cosecant (csc).

∽

The **SINE** of an angle is the ratio of the opposite side to the length of the hypotenuse. Or:

$$\sin \theta = \frac{\text{opposite of angle}}{\text{hypotenuse}}$$

∽

The **COSINE** of an angle is the ratio of the adjacent side to the length of the hypotenuse. Or:

$$\cos \theta = \frac{\text{adjacent line}}{\text{hypotenuse}}$$

∽

The **TANGENT** of an angle is the ratio of the opposite side to the length of the adjacent side. Or:

$$\tan \theta = \frac{\text{opposite of angle}}{\text{adjacent line}}$$

An easy way to remember the three formulas is: SOH-CAH-TOA. The letters correspond with the function and the ratios.

If you need to solve for a third side, and the other two sides of a triangle and the angle are known, then you use the **LAW OF COSINES.** The formula for the law of cosines is:

$$c^2 = a^2 + b^2 - 2ab \cos \theta$$

For example, if we are given a triangle ABC, side $a = 9$ inches, side $b = 11$ inches, and the angle of C is $60°$, what is the value of c? The formula would look like this:

$$c^2 = 9^2 + 11^2 - 2(9)(11) \cos 60$$

$$c^2 = 202 - 99$$

$$c^2 = 103$$

$$c = \sqrt{103}$$

For the **LAW OF SINES**, we are considering triangles where the sides are the same ratio as the sines of opposite angles. So $a : b : c = \sin A : \sin B : \sin C$. So, side a is to b, as $\sin A$ is to $\sin B$, and the same with b to c. In other words:

$$\frac{a}{b} = \frac{\sin A}{\sin B} \quad \text{and} \quad \frac{b}{c} = \frac{\sin B}{\sin C}$$

ဟ

IDENTITIES are true no matter what value the variable is. For example, the problem $(x + 3)(x - 3) = x^2 - 9$ is always true. That makes it an identity. In trigonometry, there are several reciprocal identities one has to know:

$$\sin \theta = \frac{1}{\csc \theta} \qquad\qquad \csc \theta = \frac{1}{\sin \theta}$$

$$\cos \theta = \frac{1}{\sec \theta} \qquad\qquad \sec \theta = \frac{1}{\cos \theta}$$

$$\tan \theta = \frac{1}{\cot \theta} \qquad\qquad \cot \theta = \frac{1}{\tan \theta}$$

ဟ

When given the value of a function and asked to find the value of the angle, it is referred to as an **INVERSE TRIGONOMETRIC FUNCTION**. The terms used for inverse functions are *arcsin, arccos, arctan, arccot, arcsec,* and *arccsc.* If $f(x) = \sin x$ and $g(x) = \arcsin x$, then the formula for finding the inverse trigonometric functions is $f(g(x)) = x$ or $g(f(x)) = x$. So arcsin $x = y$, which leads us to the formula $x = \sin y$.

ဟ

The arc length of a circle is defined as a **RADIAN**. One revolution in a circle is measured as 2π. This means that half of a circle is π, and that every right angle in a circle is $\pi/2$. $\pi/4$ is half of a right angle, and thus equals 45°. So this means that 2π is actually 360°. To find degrees in radians, the equation you have to follow is:

$$\text{Radians} = \frac{\text{Degrees}}{180} \bullet \pi$$

LOGARITHMS AND *e*

The number **e**, also known as Euler's number, is one of the most famous and important irrational numbers, and it is the base of the natural logarithms. The number was introduced in the early 1600s by John Napier, who abandoned the concept of natural logarithms, and instead focused on common logarithms with a base of ten. Leonhard Euler picked up where John Napier left off, and is responsible for discovering the properties of *e*. The number e expands infinitely, with the first values of *e* being:

$$e = 2.71828182845904523536\ldots$$

ᔕ

Maybe the most useful concept in arithmetic that can be used in all sciences, **LOGARITHMS** provide a way to express the power that a fixed base, or number, is raised to so that a given answer is produced. Common logarithms have a base of 10, while **NATURAL LOGARITHMS** have a base *e*. Here are some basic logs:

log(10) = 1	This is because $10^1 = 10$
log(100) = 2	This is because $10^2 = 100$
log(2) ≈ 0.3	This is because $10^{0.3} = 2$

ᔕ

The opposite of a log, known as an **ANTILOG**, looks like this: antilog(2) = 100. With antilogs, you are just raising the base (10) to the power of x (in this case 2).

ᔕ

Just like you can add exponents when there is the same base, logarithms follow a similar rule. Here are the three main rules for logarithms (note: these only work when the bases are identical):

- When adding logs with the same base, multiply the numbers inside the logs:

$$\log_b(m) + \log_b(n) = \log_b(mn)$$

- When subtracting logs with the same base, divide the numbers inside the logs:

$$\log_b(m) - \log_b(n) = \log_b(m/n)$$

- When there is a multiplier, it turns into an exponent for everything inside the log, and vice versa:

$$n \bullet \log_b(m) = \log_b(m^n)$$

EXTRACURRICULARS: STUDENT COUNCIL

Through his popular blog *FiveThirtyEight* writer and statistician **NATE SILVER** has been tracking sports statistics and election data. Using polling and forecasting, Silver has become a master of predicting elections, and correctly chose Barack Obama as the winner in 2008 and 2012.

SENIOR YEAR: CALCULUS

LIMITS

CALCULUS is the study of change over time using advanced forms of geometry and algebra, and it has many real-world applications. It provides the framework to understand why things change, how to model things, and how to predict change in models. Calculus deals with the concept of **INFINITY**. If something is always changing, it is changing infinitely.

LIMITS are the intended height of a particular function. The formula for limits looks like this:

$$\lim_{x \to c} f(x) = n$$

Limits deal with the process of moving up the graph, and are not concerned with the value of c.

There are essentially four ways to determine a limit as x approaches a given value:

1. You can examine the graphical behavior of a function.
2. You can carefully draw conclusions from a table.
3. You can take a numerical approach, almost creating your own table of values.
4. You can take an analytic approach, which usually involves simplification of the function and direct substitution of a value.

If a function is said to be **CONTINUOUS** at a certain point (c), it must fulfill three requirements:

- $\lim_{x \to c} k(x)$ exists.

- $k(c)$ exists.

- $\lim_{x \to c} k(x) = k(c)$.

The **INTERMEDIATE VALUE THEOREM** states that if $w(x)$ is continuous on the closed interval $[a,b]$, and k is any value such that $w(a) \leq k \leq w(b)$, then there exists at least one value c in $[a,b]$ such that $w(c) = k$. This is also true if $w(b) \leq k \leq w(a)$.

MAXIMA and **MINIMA** (known as extrema) are the largest and smallest values a function has within a specific area (local), or as a whole (global or absolute). Local maximum is the height at a point that is greater than or equal to any other points in the interval. The formula for local maximum is $f(a) \geq f(x)$. Local minimum is the opposite, with a formula of: $f(a) \leq f(x)$.

DIFFERENTIATION

The **DERIVATIVE** is one of the core concepts used in calculus. In calculus, derivatives are represented in two ways. In geometric terms, derivatives represent the slope of a line. The other way to show a derivative is physically, as the **RATE OF CHANGE**. In a straight line, the slope indicates the speed at which the function changes. With a curved line, however, the slope changes, and this is where derivatives are used.

DIFFERENTIATION is the process of finding the derivatives. There are several rules of differentiation. Among these rules are the **CONSTANT RULE**, which states if $f(x) = c$, then $f'(x) = 0$ (for example, if $f(x) = 5$, then $f'(x) = 0$) and the **POWER RULE**, which states $f(x) = nx^{n-1}$, where n equals the exponent. For example, if $f(x) = x^4$, then $f'(x) = 4x^3$.

To find the **AVERAGE RATE OF CHANGE**: Let $f(t)$ be any function. The average rate of change of $f(t)$ on the interval $[t_1, t_2]$ is calculated by applying the formula:

$$R_{avg} = \frac{\Delta f}{\Delta t} = \frac{f(t_2) - f(t_1)}{t_2 - t_1}$$

The symbol Δ (the Greek capital letter delta) is a math and science shorthand notation for "change in." For example, Δf is read "change in f." This expression is called a difference quotient:

$$\frac{\Delta f}{\Delta t} = \frac{f(t_2) - f(t_1)}{t_2 - t_1}$$

You always calculate an average rate of change over an interval of time and use subtraction to do so. The word *average* may make you think you must add, but the real emphasis is on change. Change is measured by finding differences. Remember that average rate of change is simply slope, and slope is the difference of the dependent variables divided by the difference of the independent variables.

Your average change at a point in time is known as **INSTANTANE-OUS RATE OF CHANGE**, and can be calculated as follows. Let $f(t)$ be any function. The instantaneous rate of change of $f(t)$ at any given moment is calculated by:

$$R_{inst} = \lim_{\Delta t \to 0} \frac{\Delta f}{\Delta t}$$

An important difference is that an average rate of change is calculated over an interval, whereas an instantaneous rate of change is calculated at a point in time.

To use this information to calculate a derivative, you can use the following calculation: Let $y = f(x)$ be any function continuous on some interval containing a point $[c, f(c)]$. If it can be calculated, the derivative of $y = f(x)$ at a point $x = c$ is:

$$\lim_{\Delta x \to 0} \frac{\Delta y}{\Delta x} = \lim_{\Delta x \to 0} \frac{f(c + \Delta x) - f(c)}{\Delta x}$$

If the derivative exists, then f is said to be **DIFFERENTIABLE**. The derivative of $f(x)$ at $x = c$ is the slope of f at c.

Another way to consider the definition of a derivative is to let f be a continuous function on an interval containing a known point $[a, f(a)]$, and let $[x, f(x)]$ be any general point on the graph of the function. The derivative of f at a is:

$$\lim_{x \to a} \frac{f(x) - f(a)}{x - a}$$

Some common derivatives:

- The derivative of x is 1.
- The derivative of x^2 is $2x$, x^3 is $3x^2$, x^4 is $4x^3$, etc.
- The derivative of $\sin(x)$ is $\cos(x)$, and of $\cos(x)$ is $-\sin(x)$.

INTEGRATION

INTEGRATION in calculus deals with two things. The first is to find the **ANTIDERIVATIVE**, which is the inverse transform of the derivative. The other thing integration does is find the value of the area below the curve. Integration is represented by $\int f(x)\,dx$. And dx equals the difference of x_n and x_{n-1}. Two common equations for integration are:

$$\text{If } f(x) = x^n, \text{ then } f(x)\,dx = x^{n+1}/(n+1)$$

$$\text{If } f(x) = cx^n, \text{ then } f(x)\,dx = cx^{n+1}/(n+1)$$

∽

THE FUNDAMENTAL THEOREM OF CALCULUS links the concept of the derivative with that of the integral. It is separated into two parts:

∽

The first part asserts that the instantaneous rate of change of the integral of any function is the function itself: Let f be any continuous function, and let a be a constant. Then:

$$\frac{d}{dx}\left[\int_a^x f(t)dt\right] = f(x)$$

∽

The second part states: Let g be any antiderivative of the continuous function f on the interval $[a,b]$. Then:

$$\int_a^b f(t)dt = g(b) - g(a)$$

Find the antiderivative of the integrand evaluated at the upper limit minus the antiderivative evaluated at the lower limit.

∽

In other words these calculations allow us to determine the area underneath the curve at a certain interval, and find a way to bring together the two major pieces of calculus—the derivative and the integral.

INFINITY

The symbol for **INFINITY**, ∞, is known as a lemniscate. This comes from the Latin word *lemniscus*, which means "ribbon." In John Wallis's *Treatise on the Conic Sections* published in 1655, the symbol is used for the very first time. It is unknown why Wallis chose the symbol.

∽

There are some basic formulas regarding infinity, indicating its limitlessness. For example, $x \rightarrow \infty$ and $x \rightarrow -\infty$ show that x can grow and decrease without bound. If every t is $f(t) \geq 0$, then:

$$\int_{-\infty}^{\infty} f(t) \, dt = \infty$$
shows the area under $f(t)$ is infinite

$$\int_{-\infty}^{\infty} f(t) \, dt = n$$
shows that the area under $f(t)$ equals n, and thus, is finite

$$\int_{a}^{b} f(t) \, dt = \infty$$
shows $f(t)$ doesn't bound an area that is finite from a to b

∽

GALILEO came up with a surprising paradox relating to infinity. Galileo noticed that if you remove half of the set of equal numbers, there are as many numbers remaining in the set as before. For example, if you remove all of the odd numbers from a set, you will only have the even numbers remaining. If you then pair the natural numbers (n) with $2n$ (which is even) the set that has the even numbers is equinumerous (meaning they have the same cardinality) to the set that had all natural numbers. In other words, if you had infinity, you still have infinity.

∽

GEORG CANTOR came to the realization that one cannot count to infinity, but one can compare sets to see if they are the same size by finding a one-to-one matching of the elements within the sets. The size of any set is known as cardinality. Sets are known as infinite if elements can be removed without reducing the cardinality. When there is the same cardinality as there are natural numbers, the set is called countable. Cantor's theorem states if there is a set X, there is at least one set that is raised to the power of X, and that is cardinally greater than X.

EXTRACURRICULARS: DRAMA CLUB

RUSSELL CROWE and **MATT DAMON** were both nominated for Academy Awards for playing mathematicians, Crowe in *A Beautiful Mind*, which won Best Picture in 2002, and Damon in *Good Will Hunting*, which won the Oscar for Best Original Screenplay in 1998.

PERIOD 7
PHILOSOPHY

PHILOSOPHY IS THE STUDY OF OUR MOST FUNDAMENTAL BELIEFS and the rational grounds underlying the concepts of being and thinking. The word *philosophy* comes from the Greek *philosophia* meaning "love of wisdom." So if you love to learn (or if you forget if you once did), this is the class for you. Plus, you'll sound smart if you can quote Sartre at a party.

FRESHMAN YEAR: GREEK PHILOSOPHY

THE ORIGINS OF PHILOSOPHY

Philosophy in the Western world began in ancient Greece with Thales, Anaximander, and Anaximenes. These three philosophers differed from earlier approaches by explaining the world with natural rather than divine causes.

ꙅ

THALES (ca. 625–545 B.C.E.) was a man of broad interests in science and mathematics and likely traveled to Egypt to learn practical skills. He eschewed supernatural or mystical explanations for the world around him and tried to give rational explanations for natural phenomena. Thales believed that water was the source of all things and also subscribed to the doctrine of hylozoism, the theory that all matter possesses life or can feel sensations.

ꙅ

ANAXIMANDER (ca. 610–545 B.C.E.) was a student of Thales and is known for inventing the sundial and providing the first map of the Greek world. Anaximander disagreed with his teacher and contended that the original substance of the universe was not matter like water, but rather must have been something more immaterial. He thought the fundamental, ultimate stuff of the universe must be the infinite.

ꙅ

ANAXIMENES (ca. 585–525 B.C.E.) said that cosmic air, or mist, extended everywhere, pervading all things in the universe, and was the primordial element.

THE PRE-SOCRATICS

PYTHAGORAS (ca. 580–500 B.C.E.), one of the most celebrated and controversial of the ancient Greek philosophers and mathematicians, founded a brotherhood of disciples known for their belief in the purification of the soul. He believed in reincarnation, that all living things must be interrelated, and that mathematical principles could explain all of reality.

§

Pythagoras is traditionally credited with the first use of the term *philosophy*.

§

Members of the Pythagorean school believed in following strict moral, ascetic, and dietary rules to enable their souls to reach a higher level and be liberated from the "wheel of birth." They also believed that numbers were the essence of all things. These early Greeks tried to understand the world in a rational manner and did not think that natural events were determined by the wills of gods. They laid the groundwork for later philosophers by questioning where things came from.

§

HERACLITUS (540–480 B.C.E.) changed the focus of early Greek philosophy from emphasis on the ultimate constituents of the world to the problem of change. His main contribution to philosophy is his thought that unity exists in diversity, that reality is one and many at the same time.

§

Contrary to Heraclitus, **PARMENIDES** (ca. 515–450 B.C.E.) thought that all change is an illusion of the senses. The same is true of diversity and motion: they are unreal appearances.

Like Parmenides, **ZENO** (ca. 490–430 B.C.E.) took the view that common sense led to absurd conclusions.

SOCRATES

Without writing a single word, **SOCRATES** (ca. 470–399 B.C.E.) is arguably the most important philosopher in the history of Western thought. His philosophical mission began with an oracle, or divinely appointed authority, who declared him the wisest living person. He set out to disprove the oracle and went about Athens questioning others, concluding that: "Real wisdom is the property of God."

Socrates thought that philosophy ought to be concerned with practical questions about how to live and the nature of the good life. Because of these concerns about values, he essentially invented the field of philosophy known as **ETHICS**.

One of Socrates's lasting contributions to philosophy is his skillful method of cross-examination. What is now known as the **SOCRATIC METHOD**, a form of debate that has two opposing parties ask and answer questions, was his manner of attaining knowledge. The method was designed to force one to examine one's beliefs and the validity of such beliefs.

Socrates sought definitions of terms like *justice* and *virtue, love* and *piety*. He thought that one couldn't know what love and virtue were unless one could define these terms. He used inductive reasoning, starting with particular statements like "This generous action is virtuous," hoping to establish more important generalizations like "All generous actions are virtuous."

PLATO

Born in Athens, **PLATO** (ca. 428–348 B.C.E.) was twenty-nine years old when his teacher Socrates died. In the course of his lengthy life, Plato used dialogues, an inherently dramatic form, to pour forth a complete system of philosophy, and made contributions to every branch of philosophy, leaving behind a system of thought that is breathtaking in its breadth and depth.

ഗ

In 387 B.C.E., Plato founded the **ACADEMY** in Athens for the study of philosophy, mathematics, logic, the sciences, and legislative, political, and ethical ideas. The Academy lasted for several centuries after his death and is regarded by many to have been the first university.

ഗ

Plato believed that engaging with ideas he called forms—chief among these being justice, beauty, and equality—would lead to the understanding necessary for a good life.

ഗ

Plato attempted to show the rational relationship between the soul, the state, and the universe, and built a systematic, rational treatment of the forms and their interrelations, starting with the supreme idea of Good. He believed that people could, through constant questioning, achieve understanding.

The first group of the **DIALOGUES OF PLATO** includes those early writings that consider moral excellence. These ideas were also held by Socrates, and included pursuing definitions of courage, piety, friendship, and self-control.

The middle group of dialogues includes Plato's theory of forms and accompanying theory of knowledge, his account of the human soul, his political ideas, and his ideas about art. Most notable among the middle dialogues is the incomparable **THE REPUBLIC**, his treatise on the nature of justice.

The third and final group of writings is what now might be called meta-philosophical. These dialogues are highly technical, showing a concern for logical and linguistic issues.

ARISTOTLE

ARISTOTLE (384–322 B.C.E.) was a student of Plato's and a member of his Academy. In 335 B.C.E. he founded **THE LYCEUM**, a school in Athens that he also directed for twelve years, which was also known as the Peripatetic school for its scholars' habit of walking about.

Aristotle delved into many subjects, including metaphysics, logic, aesthetics, ethics, and political thought, and is regarded as one of the most influential figures in the history of Western philosophy.

Aristotle was the first person to systematize the rules of logic, the specifics of which can be found in his **ORGANON**. He was chiefly concerned with the form of proof and was most interested in **SYLLOGISM**, which he assumed provided certain knowledge concerning reality gained by logical deduction.

There are three laws of thought according to Aristotle:

1. **THE PRINCIPLE OF CONTRADICTION:** Asserts that a statement cannot be true and false at the same time.
2. **THE PRINCIPLE OF THE EXCLUDED MIDDLE:** Declared that a statement must be true or false; there is no "middle" possibility.
3. **THE PRINCIPLE OF IDENTITY:** States that everything is equal to itself.

Aristotle thought that the true philosopher is one who desires knowledge about the ultimate causes and nature of reality and desires that knowledge for its own sake, not for any practical use.

EXTRACURRICULARS: YEARBOOK
MOST LIKELY TO HAVE A CONVERSATION WITH HIMSELF

Around 380 B.C.E. Plato published *The Republic* as a dialogue with Socrates and others about the ideas of justice and order for city-states and for men. The book has been the subject of entire college seminars, and continues to inspire philosophers and philosophy students today.

SOPHOMORE YEAR: MEDIEVAL AND RENAISSANCE PHILOSOPHY

MEDIEVAL PHILOSOPHERS

The predominant system of theological and philosophical teaching in medieval times was known as **SCHOLASTICISM**.

ળ

Two fundamental problems persisted during this period, which lasted from 529 to 1453. The first was the problem of universals, or whether ideas could exist apart from things themselves. The second problem was devising logical proofs for the existence of God.

ળ

During the medieval period, philosophy was often viewed as "**THE HANDMAIDEN OF FAITH**." Philosophy could be used to help establish beliefs by making use of reason and argument. When conflict arose between the claims of faith and the claims of reason, that conflict got resolved in favor of faith.

ળ

SAINT ANSELM OF CANTERBURY (1033–1109) was an Italian who became the abbot of a monastery in Normandy and was made archbishop of Canterbury in 1093. Anselm tried to provide rational support for the doctrines of Christianity, assuming no boundaries between reason and faith. He thought that natural theology—that is, basing conclusions about God's existence on logical arguments—could provide a rational version of what he already believed.

AVICENNA (980–1037) was a Muslim philosopher who also thought that God's essence necessarily implied his existence. He coupled Saint Anselm with Aristotle to arrive at his own doctrine of Creation: God is at the apex of being, has no beginning, is always active (in the Aristotelian sense of never being merely potential but always expressing his full being), and therefore has always created. According to Avicenna, then, creation is both necessary and eternal.

PETER ABÉLARD (1079–1142) was a French theologian and philosopher whose most famous work, *Sic et Non* (Yes and No), exhibited a style of dialectical discussion by setting out more than 150 theological questions to challenge students.

WILLIAM OF OCKHAM (ca. 1280–1349), an English Franciscan friar, is known for **OCCAM'S RAZOR,** or the principle of parsimony. The principle of Occam's razor reflects the idea that if you possess two different theories explaining some scientific data, you should choose the one that puts forward the minimum number of assumptions. In other words, Ockham thought that the simplest solution was often the correct one.

SAINT THOMAS AQUINAS (1225–1274) was a prolific writer whose reputation is based largely on his ability to take Aristotle's philosophy—by the thirteenth century translated into Latin across Europe—and join it to Christian thought. Aquinas's philosophy is grounded in Aristotle. His terminology of form and matter, substance and accident, and actuality and potentiality, is the very framework Aristotle employed to express his ideas about objects in nature.

RENAISSANCE THINKERS

Technology was essential to the Renaissance. The invention of the printing press in the mid-1400s made the works of great authors widely available.

∽

Under Cosimo de' Medici, forty-five copyists working feverishly for two years had produced just 200 volumes; by the year 1500 some thousand printers had produced over 9 million books.

∽

There are two phases to the Renaissance: the humanistic phase and the natural science phase. The arts and philosophy in the **HUMAN-ISTIC PHASE** of the Renaissance (from 1453 to 1600) were human-centered, emphasizing the place of humans in the universe.

∽

The key thinkers of the humanistic period were Desiderius Erasmus and Martin Luther.

∽

DESIDERIUS ERASMUS (1466–1536) celebrated the human spirit in his writings and saw no tension between the classics and religious faith. While his work inspired the Protestant reformers to follow his lead—especially Martin Luther, with whom Erasmus feuded—he wished to heal, not break, the church.

∽

MARTIN LUTHER (1483–1546) was outraged by the church's policy of charging a monetary fee for the sacrament of confession—what he thought of as the selling of indulgences—and nailed his famous

NINETY-FIVE THESES to the door of the Castle Church of Wittenberg in 1517. In time his bold action would incite a major protest against the Church—the Protestant Reformation—that would be felt across Europe. In undercutting the religious authority of the Catholic church, downplaying subservience to tradition, and placing new importance on the individual, the Reformation caused a groundswell against all intellectual authorities and traditions.

ᔕ

NICCOLÒ MACHIAVELLI (1469–1527) is undoubtedly the most important political philosopher of the era and is best known for **THE PRINCE**, a work he viewed as an objective view of political reality: "The ends justify the means."

ᔕ

Philosophy during the **NATURAL SCIENCE** period (from 1600 to 1690) was cosmos-centered.

ᔕ

The significant figures of the natural science period were scientific thinkers, Nicolaus Copernicus, a mathematician and astronomer, and Galileo Galilei, a central figure in the scientific revolution, in particular.

ᔕ

On his deathbed, the Polish astronomer **NICOLAUS COPERNICUS** (1473–1543) published his work that placed the Sun at the center of our solar system. This work famously ran counter to the Ptolemaic system that placed Earth at the center of the universe, favored by the church.

GALILEO

In his time, **GALILEO** (1564–1642), the Italian astronomer, philosopher, and mathematician, took up the cause, based on his own observations of the heavens. He was subsequently condemned by Rome and placed under house arrest. His thinking and experimental methods, however, became the basis for the scientific revolution in seventeenth-century Europe.

ᔕ

In 1609, Galileo heard news of an invention in the Netherlands that would make faraway objects appear close—the spyglass. Determined to figure out how the invention worked, Galileo tried making his own, and in only twenty-four hours, without ever having seen the object and going by only the rumors he had heard, he created a three-power telescope. After making some changes, he brought the now ten-power **TELESCOPE** to the Venetian Senate and demonstrated how it worked.

ᔕ

During Galileo's time, the widespread belief was that the Moon was actually completely smooth and polished. As Galileo focused his new invention on the Moon, he began noticing a surface that was anything but smooth. The landscape of the Moon was rough, full of cavities and craters, and uneven. People dismissed Galileo's findings, and some even argued that the surface of the Moon was covered with an invisible layer of smooth crystal.

ᔕ

By January of 1610, Galileo fixed his telescope on the stars and began to focus on Jupiter, noticing three bright stars in a straight line near the planet. When looking the following evening, the three stars had moved to the west of the planet, while still maintaining the straight line. Over time, Galileo came to the conclusion that these were satellites of Jupiter that rotated around the planet. If satellites rotated around another planet, perhaps the Earth was not the center of the universe as many believed.

∽

Galileo continued to study the planets, and his findings started to contradict the beliefs of the church. Galileo was, in fact, quite religious, but he believed the Bible should not be taken so literally. This led to charges of heresy from the church. He was eventually found innocent; however, sixteen years later he was put under house arrest until his death for a book he had written expressing Copernican theory.

> **EXTRACURRICULARS: STUDENT COUNCIL**
> Though Machiavelli's *The Prince* gets a bad rap as a treatise on the end justifying the means, as often applied to politics, the philosopher saw the works as a handbook for those who seek political power. The term *Machiavellian* has become synonymous with cunning, deceit, and ruthlessness; however many have used the work as inspiration for gaining and remaining in power in the 500 years since its publication.

JUNIOR YEAR: EMPIRICISM AND EARLY MODERN PHILOSOPHY

EARLY EMPIRICISM

EMPIRICISM (which comes from a Greek word *empeiria*, meaning "experience") was a philosophy that stated all knowledge begins with experience.

Following the Renaissance, two forerunners of a scientific, experience-based philosophy were Francis Bacon and Thomas Hobbes.

∽

SIR FRANCIS BACON (1561–1626) was an English philosopher, essayist, and statesman. After a failed career as public servant, Bacon spent his last years working on the reform of learning and the establishment of community dedicated to the discovery of scientific knowledge.

∽

In **THE NEW ORGANON**, Bacon introduces his doctrine of the idols that impede knowledge:

- **THE IDOLS OF THE TRIBE** are innate human weaknesses, such as the tendency to trust one's senses or to discern more order in events than actually exists.
- **THE IDOLS OF THE CAVE** vary between individuals and include prejudices or distortions due to unique backgrounds.
- **THE IDOLS OF THE MARKETPLACE** hinder clear thinking and are due to imprecise language.
- **THE IDOLS OF THE THEATER** derive from grand systems of philosophy.

∽

Bacon was opposed to the rationalist tendency inherent in Plato's teachings that examined the content and meaning of words to attain knowledge. He also made attacks on Aristotle, the other giant of the classical period, for amassing data but making no scientific hypotheses.

∽

THOMAS HOBBES (1588–1679) became one of the great seventeenth-century philosophers. In **LEVIATHAN** (1651), Hobbes claimed that the physical motions of objects in the external world produce human sensations, and all events in nature and all behavior is determined.

ॐ

Hobbes said that people are egoistic hedonists, always guided by their own pursuit of pleasure. Hence, people are unfailingly self-interested and therefore psychologically determined to seek their own pleasure. Because people live in a state characterized by fear and violence, self-interest compels them to create a government with a strong ruler.

ॐ

Hobbes's reputation as an important thinker in many areas remains and he has been referred to as the founder of **MODERN POLITICAL SCIENCE**.

DESCARTES AND MODERN PHILOSOPHY

RENÉ DESCARTES (1596–1650), French mathematician and philosopher, received a Jesuit education, traveled widely for ten years, and finally settled in Holland. Descartes is recognized as the father of modern philosophy for his break with medieval thinking and using the methodology of the sciences to establish a rational foundation for truth.

ॐ

Descartes's philosophy centered on three goals:

1. To eliminate doubt and find certainty.
2. To find a set of principles, or starting points, from which he could deduce all answers to scientific questions.
3. To reconcile his mechanistic view of the universe with his own religious perspective. If the world was a deterministic machine, as Hobbes and other materialists had argued, then how would there

be room for human freedom? What need was there for God in such a universe?

∽

Descartes methodically questions all knowledge, whatever its basis. He then goes on to construct something about which he can be certain: because Descartes doubts, he exists. He states: **COGITO ERGO SUM** (I think, therefore I am).

∽

Descartes believed that the mind and the body were distinct, and he called this idea **MIND-BODY DUALISM**.

NEWTON AND LOCKE

SIR ISAAC NEWTON (1642–1727) and **JOHN LOCKE** (1632–1704) were Enlightenment philosophers. Thinkers during the European Enlightenment were confident that man could solve his problems— problems of government, morals, and society included—by the use of reason. Even the universe could be mathematically understood.

∽

Newton's genius had manifested by his early twenties. He made significant discoveries in mathematics and physics from 1664 to 1667, but his masterpiece, commonly known as **THE PRINCIPIA**, appeared in 1687.

∽

This important work set forth the mathematical laws of physics and "the system of the world." Newton had always insisted on adherence to experimental observation and induction for advancing scientific knowledge, and he rejected speculative metaphysics. He believed nature would be revealed through mathematical treatment.

John Locke's legacy is vast: he was a notable political, economic, and religious thinker. He was a **LATITUDINARIAN**, one who conformed to the Church of England but placed little importance on the church's doctrine or practices. He was a broad churchman in theology and a liberal in politics.

He argued against the authority of the Bible and the church. Locke maintained that political sovereignty depended upon the consent of the governed and ecclesiastical authority upon the consent of reason.

Locke's political theory (set forth in 1690 in his *Two Treatises of Government*) defended the doctrine of human liberty and human rights against absolutism. These principles were incorporated into the Constitution of the United States.

HUME AND KANT

DAVID HUME (1711–1776) was a Scottish philosopher and historian who took empirical philosophy further than did Locke. He applied it relentlessly to issues of how people attain knowledge, to beliefs about God and miracles, and to moral philosophy. When he was twenty-eight, he published his first and greatest philosophical work, *A TREATISE OF HUMAN NATURE* (1739).

Hume tried to describe how the mind acquires knowledge, which he divided into matters of fact and relations of ideas.

Hume was a skeptic about God's existence. The existence of the universe is surely an empirical fact, but he thought the existence of God could not be inferred from it since people have neither an impression of God nor of the alleged act of Creation.

∽

David Hume laid the groundwork for the skepticism and strict empiricism of the twentieth century. Hume gave philosophy the impetus to question any and all statements that could not be substantiated with reason or by exacting tests of experience.

∽

IMMANUEL KANT (1724–1804) achieved a synthesis of empiricism and rationalist thought. He claimed that knowledge was impossible without accepting truths from both rationalist and empiricist schools. He based his ethics on reason and said that moral duties could be deduced by all rational beings.

∽

Kant believed that humans are active in knowing the world. Although all our knowledge begins with experience, it does not follow that all of it arises out of that experience.

EXTRACURRICULARS: DRAMA CLUB

Ayn Rand (1905–1982) was a philosopher and author of novels like *The Fountainhead* and *Atlas Shrugged*. Her philosophy rejected altruism, and supported egoism. In 1999, Helen Mirren played Rand in the Showtime original movie *The Passion of Ayn Rand* and won an Emmy Award for the portrayal.

Kant proposed that the mind has categories of understanding which catalog, codify, and make sense of the world. The mind cannot experience anything that is not filtered through the mind's eye and, therefore, can never know the true nature of reality. In this sense, Kant claimed that perception is reality.

SENIOR YEAR: NINETEENTH- AND TWENTIETH-CENTURY PHILOSOPHY

EXISTENTIALISM

EXISTENTIALISM is the philosophical study of the meaning of existence. There are several key ideas that existentialism touches on, such as free will, the idea that human nature is made by the choices one makes in life, the idea that decisions create stress and have consequences, and that people are at their best when struggling for life. Existentialism is very much about understanding the meaning of life on a personal level without touching on factors like wealth, social values, or other external forces.

ᗰ

SØREN KIERKEGAARD (1813–1855) was born in Copenhagen, Denmark, and his philosophy, by contrast to the grand systems built by Plato and Aristotle, stressed the existing individual and how he lived in the world day to day.

Kierkegaard said that truth is subjectivity; there is no prefabricated truth for people who make choices. Kierkegaard had a higher regard for **SUBJECTIVE TRUTH** than **OBJECTIVE TRUTH**. It is the factor that makes Kierkegaard the **"FATHER" OF EXISTENTIALISM**.

The individual acts on truth, he maintained, and this truth was a manner of existence. Man exists in his truth and lives in it. The highest expression of subjectivity is passionate belief. This is what it means to think existentially.

The essence of Kierkegaard's philosophy can be seen in his three stages of life experience:

- **AESTHETIC:** A stage of living for the moment, the continual search for diversion, and ultimate futility.
- **ETHICAL:** The stage of decision and resolute commitment in which the individual accepts responsibility and follows rules of conduct.
- **RELIGIOUS:** The stage of obedience and commitment to God. This is a personal, subjective experience and relationship, and is, in Kierkegaard's view, a leap of faith.

Kierkegaard's life and philosophy were centered on existential questions:

- *How shall I live my life?*
- *What kind of life is worth living—the aesthetic, ethical, or religious?*
- *What does it mean to have faith?*
- *What does it mean to love?*
- *What does it mean to accept one's suffering and how can one do this?*

PRAGMATISM

PRAGMATISM is an antisystematic, antiempirical, and antirationalist philosophy that grew up in America in the nineteenth century. The practical consequences and meanings of ideas in the real world were more important to pragmatists than the theoretical coherence of some of the systematic philosophies of the past.

∽

Although **CHARLES SANDERS PEIRCE** (1839–1914) was the "father" of pragmatism, **WILLIAM JAMES** (1842–1910) gave the term its clearest expression. James insisted that all knowledge is pragmatic because it is difficult if not impossible to settle some philosophical questions—like whether there is a God or an afterlife. James thought that it was best to believe the theory that brings about the best consequences in one's life.

∽

Peirce founded an organization known as the **METAPHYSICAL CLUB** that met in the 1870s in Cambridge, Massachusetts, to read and debate philosophical papers. The better-known members of this group included Peirce, William James, and future Supreme Court justice Oliver Wendell Holmes, Jr.

∽

Pragmatism offered an altogether relaxed attitude about what is true, meaningful, and significant in people's lives.

∽

Pragmatism opposed doctrines that believed truth could be reached through deductive reasoning from a priori grounds. In contrast, it held that truth changes as discoveries are made and is relative to the time, place, and purpose of inquiry. What difference beliefs make is more obvious—and in some ways more important—than whether those beliefs are true.

ANALYTIC PHILOSOPHY

ANALYTIC PHILOSOPHY, also known as linguistic philosophy, was a twentieth-century philosophical movement especially strong in England and the United States. Analytic philosophy concentrated on language—making it unambiguous and concise—and the attempt to analyze statements in order to clarify philosophical problems.

တ

Philosophers thought science had taken over much of the territory formerly occupied by philosophy, but **MORITZ SCHLICK**, an early member of the analytic movement, believed that science should be defined as the pursuit of truth and philosophy as the pursuit of meaning.

တ

New and more powerful methods of logic that developed in the twentieth century promised to shed new light on some of the old, philosophical stalemates by eliminating propositions that were vague, equivocal, misleading, or nonsensical.

တ

BERTRAND RUSSELL (1872–1970) touched almost every area of philosophy and made major contributions to mathematics and logical analysis. His theory of definite descriptions maintained that sentences were descriptions consisting of a conjunction of separate entities. Each of the entities can be tested to determine if it's true.

Logically, any statement that is a conjunction of entities is false if any one of the entities is false. Russell's theory of definite descriptions shows that it is possible to speak sensibly of things that do not exist. Since Russell, it has become a standard tool of logical analysis.

∽

There is little question that analytic philosophy changed the manner in which philosophers worked. Using newer methods of logical and linguistic analysis illuminated old philosophical queries in ethics, metaphysics, and epistemology.

SARTRE AND METAPHYSICS

JEAN-PAUL SARTRE (1905–1980) eventually became the leading voice of atheistic existentialism.

∽

In his essay **"EXISTENTIALISM IS A HUMANISM"** (1946), Sartre set forth a novel idea of human freedom. He used the phrase "existence precedes essence," which says that there is no such thing as a given human nature.

∽

On the contrary, personal choices and acts make up one's identity. Man first exists, and his choices then define his essence: individuals give meaning to facts by deciding how to act. Sartre also rejected the existence of God by pointing out that people are free agents, and this would not be the case if God existed.

In the twentieth century, philosophers like **GILBERT RYLE, A.J. AYER**, and **ANTONY FLEW** brought new life to old metaphysical issues like mind-body interaction, God's existence, and the problem of evil.

Their revelations were more about the analysis of concepts and the language used than in introducing new content. But good analytic philosophy brought new understanding to old problems.

Contemporary ethics have added a great deal to the history of ethical thinking in at least two ways:

- There has been increased attention to the meaning of ethical terms such as fairness, justice, and goodness.
- Applied ethics including legal ethics, medical ethics, the ethics of sports, the philosophy of warfare, and medical ethics have responded to social concerns.

EXTRACURRICULARS: NEWSPAPER
SARTRE WINS NOBEL PRIZE

In 1964, Jean-Paul Sartre won the Nobel Prize for Literature for, according to the Nobel Prize committee: "his work which, rich in ideas and filled with the spirit of freedom and the quest for truth, has exerted far-reaching influence on our age." Other philosophers to have won the prize include Bertrand Russell, Albert Camus, and Henri Bergson.

PERIOD 8
FOREIGN
LANGUAGE

THANKS TO THE GLOBALIZATION OF BUSINESS and to the far reach of the Internet, the world has become smaller and smaller. And that means that you cannot afford to simply speak one language. While this class will not bring your language skills to fluency, you'll find a good primer to the history of some of the languages of the world, and some key phrases for when you're visiting other countries.

FRESHMAN YEAR: INTRODUCTION TO FOREIGN LANGUAGES

SPANISH

Spanish is an Indo-European language. The earliest ancestor of Spanish was spoken 5,000 years ago around the Black Sea.

∽

Indo-European language speakers migrated throughout the land, leading to fragmentation. With the Romanization of Spain in 218 B.C.E., Latin became the language people used, and it is the direct ancestor of Spanish and all other Romance languages.

∽

Early standard Spanish was the direct result of Alfonso X the Wise, King of Castile and León. Though Latin was partly abandoned by the previous king, Alfonso X became the first king to establish Castilian, a form of Spanish spoken in northern and central Spain, as the official language to be used in the churches, courts, official documents, and books, instead of Latin.

∽

When Christopher Columbus, backed by the Spanish Empire, came to the New World in 1492, he opened the door for the Spanish conquest of what is now known as Central America. Four hundred years of colonization of this new land by the Spanish Empire followed, which included bringing over their culture, religion, and language. The Spanish would come to control Central America, much of North America, Mexico, and much of South America.

Unlike English, in Spanish the object of your sentence can come before the verb, and the subject is part of the verb. For example, in English, we would say, "I see you." The word *you*, being the object, is at the end of the sentence. "I see you" in Spanish translates as "Te veo." The object is *te*, and *veo* is actually a combination of *I* and *see*.

Today, Spanish is the native language of 332 million people, and it is the second most popular language in the world. It is the official language of numerous countries including Spain, Colombia, Peru, Cuba, Argentina, Bolivia, Mexico, Honduras, and Costa Rica. By the 1990s, the number of people in the United States who spoke Spanish as their primary language at home was more than 17 million.

EXTRACURRICULARS: NEWSPAPER
SPANISH MOST SPOKEN LANGUAGE AFTER ENGLISH IN U.S.

According to a 2011 Pew Research Center study, nearly 40 million Americans speak Spanish at home. Eighty percent of those researched also report that they speak English very well. The next most spoken language is Chinese, with 2.8 million speakers.

There are several basic things one should know how to say when traveling in a Spanish-speaking country:

- Hello! *¡Hóla!*
- Good day. *Buenos diás.*
- Thank you very much. *Muchas gracias.*
- Good night. *Buenos noches.*

- Goodbye. *Adiós.*
- Where is the bathroom? *¿Dónde está el baño?*
- Can you help me? *¿Me podría ayudar?*
- How much does that cost? *¿Cuánto cuesta?*
- Can I get on the Internet? *¿Puedo conectarme con el internet?*

FRENCH

The roots of the French language date back to 154–125 B.C.E. when Gaul was conquered by the Romans. With the Romanization, Latin became the spoken language, causing the Gaulish language to be looked down upon and only used in more rustic areas. Eventually, the north would split from the south, leading to the creation of many distinct dialects. Over time, and due to the political prestige of the area, the dialect spoken in Paris would become the national language.

∽

French consonants are pronounced similarly to the way they are in English. However, there are two major exceptions. Consonants at the end of a word (except *c*, *r*, *f*, and *l*) are not pronounced, and unlike in English, you are not supposed to linger on consonants. They should be short and quick, so that you can move on to the next vowel. The letter *r* is also pronounced from the back of your throat.

∽

Unlike consonants, French vowels are pronounced differently than they are in English. Vowels do not form diphthongs like in English. Instead of closing the vowel with a "y" or "w" sound, the vowels stay constant, and the tongue remains tense while pronouncing them. The letters *a*, *o*, and *u* are hard vowels, and *e* and *i* are soft vowels. When followed by *m* or *n*, vowels sound nasal, meaning that when pronouncing them, air escapes both the mouth and the nose.

In French, there is always an article in front of the noun, and these change according to gender (masculine, feminine), and number (singular and plural). There are three types of articles: definite (equivalent to *the* in English), indefinite (equivalent to *a/an* in English), and partitive (used when a singular noun can represent smaller parts, such as the word *food*). The articles are:

	Definite	Indefinite	Partitive
Masculine	le	un	du
Feminine	la	une	de la
Plural	les	des	—
Before Vowel	l'	de l'	—

French is the native language for approximately 75 million people worldwide, and it is the national language for over twenty-five countries including France, Haiti, Luxembourg, and Monaco, and more than fifteen countries found in Africa. It is also one of the official languages of Canada, Switzerland, and Belgium, as well as one of the six official languages used by the United Nations today.

Here are some helpful phrases to use when traveling to a French-speaking country:

- Good morning/Good day. *Bonjour.*
- Good evening. *Bonsoir.*
- Do you speak English? *Parlez-vous anglais?*
- Thank you. *Merci.*
- How are you? *Comment allez-vous?*
- What time is it? *Quelle heure est-il?*

- I need to use the restroom. *J'ai besoin d'utiliser les toilettes.*
- Please repeat. *Répétez, s'il vous plaît.*

EXTRACURRICULARS: DRAMA CLUB

Though it's primarily an American television program, and a modest hit, *THE MENTALIST* is the most watched scripted show in France. The show stars Simon Baker as a medium who helps the FBI solve crimes.

ITALIAN

Italian, like the other Romance languages, stemmed from Vulgar Latin, and it most closely resembles Latin. Around the fourteenth century, the Tuscan dialect began to dominate as a result of the aggressive commerce centered in Florence. In 1525, Venetian linguist and lawyer Pietro Bembo set out to make the dialect spoken in fourteenth-century Florence the official language of Italian literature. The first official Italian dictionary was published in 1612.

∽

The modern Italian alphabet features fewer letters than the English alphabet. Missing from the Italian alphabet are the letters *j*, *k*, *w*, *x*, and *y*. The letters *b*, *f*, *m*, *n*, and *v* are pronounced the same way they are in English. One drastic difference when it comes to consonants is that the *h* in Italian is actually silent.

∽

Vowels in Italian are short. The letters *a*, *i*, and *u* are always pronounced in the same way. The letter *a* is pronounced like in the word *cat*; the letter *i* is like the *y* in the word *yellow*; and the *u* is pronounced as in the word *fun*. The pronunciation of the letters *e* and *o*, however, will vary depending on which part of Italy you are in and could have an open or closed sound.

In Italian, some consonants have two different pronunciations depending on the letter before it. When a *c* is followed by an *a*, *o*, *u*, or a consonant, it is pronounced with a "k" sound, such as in the word *cat*. If it is followed by an *e* or an *i*, it is pronounced with a "ch" sound. If a *g* is followed by an *a*, *o*, *u*, or a consonant, it is pronounced like it is in the word *get*. If it is followed by an *e* or and *i*, it is pronounced with a "j" sound, like in the word *gym*.

Just like the other Romance languages, nouns in Italian must have a gender and number associated with them. There are two masculine articles. The first row is used for a masculine noun that begins with a consonant, unless that word starts with a *z* or begins with *s* and another consonant. In those cases, you use the second row of masculine articles.

	Singular	Plural
Masculine	il	i
Masculine	lo	gli
Feminine	la	le
Masculine/Feminine	l'	gli/le

Here are some helpful phrases to use when traveling to Italy:

- Good morning. *Buongiorno.*
- Good evening. *Buona sera.*
- Where is the bathroom? *Dove posso trovare il bagno?*
- How much is this? *Quanto costa questo?*
- Thank you. *Grazie.*
- Do you speak English? *Parli inglese?*

- Can you help me? *Può aiutarmi?/Puoi aiutarmi?* (formal/informal)
- When does the train leave? *Quando parte il treno?*

GERMAN

German is one of the largest Indo-Germanic languages today. Though it has words based on Latin, it is not a Romance language. The closest relative of German is actually English, but it is also related to Dutch, Norwegian, Danish, and Swedish. The earliest record of the language dates back to 750. The origins of the German language are broken down into three periods: Old German, Middle German, and Modern German.

ဟ

Old German was used from 750 to 1050. Old Low German was known as Old Saxon. This was spoken by people of the northwest coast of Germany and in the Netherlands. During the barbarian invasion, or the migration period, the sound of the German language began to change. This is known as the High German consonant shift, and it's what began to distinguish Old High German from Old Saxon.

ဟ

From Old Saxon came Middle Low German. This was the language spoken around the North Sea and Baltic Sea, and it had a heavy influence on the Nordic languages. From Old High German came Middle High German, which was used from 1050 to 1350. The High and Low refer to which part of the country the people lived in. During this time, a written language developed and Middle High German replaced Latin in official writings.

ဟ

Modern German began around 1500 and is still being used today. In 1880, the first grammatical rules were established, and in 1901, these were declared the standards for the German language. It is now the official language used in the church, state, education, and the arts.

∽

Today, German is the most widely spoken language in the European Union, and it is one of the three most learned languages. It is the official language of Germany, Austria, and Liechtenstein, and parts of Belgium, Luxembourg/Switzerland, France, and Italy. German is spoken by more than 100 million people worldwide.

∽

Here are helpful phrases when traveling to a German-speaking country:

- Good morning. *Guten morgen.*
- Hi. *Hallo.*
- I'm lost. *Ich habe mich verlaufen.*
- Where is the bathroom? *Wo ist das Badezimmer?*
- How much is this? *Was kostet das?/Wie teuer ist das?* (formal/informal)
- Do you speak English? *Sprechen Sie Englisch?*
- What time is it? *Wieviel Uhr ist es?/Wie spät ist es?* (formal/informal)

SOPHOMORE YEAR: INTERMEDIATE LANGUAGES

LATIN

Latin is an Indo-European language that was spoken in ancient Rome. It is the ancestor of all modern Romance languages today, including Italian, Spanish, French, Portuguese, and Romanian just to name a few. Although it is officially a dead language, meaning no one speaks it as a native language, Latin is still used in the Roman Catholic Church.

ဢ

Classical Latin was used by the ancient Romans at the same time as Archaic Latin. Classical Latin was based on the language that was spoken by the more refined, upper classes of Romans, and was found in the literature of the time. Around 75 B.C.E. to 14 C.E., dating from the Republic until the reign of Augustus Caesar, Latin literature was at its peak and was written in Classical Latin. This was referred to as the Golden Age.

ဢ

Vulgar Latin, not Classical Latin, is the closest ancestor to the Romance languages. Vulgar Latin was the Latin spoken by the common people, and was a simpler form of Classical Latin, which was used mostly in literature. Vulgar Latin varied across the Roman Empire due to the influence of the languages of local populations. By the time the Roman Empire disintegrated after 600 C.E., the local forms of Vulgar Latin were so distinct, they became the Romance languages.

ဢ

Medieval Latin was the form of Latin used in the Middle Ages, from 500 to 1500 C.E.. While it was primarily used by the Roman Catholic Church, it was also found in literature, law, administration, and science. The major distinction found in the Latin used at this time is that it began to have a wider vocabulary, grammar, and syntax, influenced by the various languages of the time.

ဢ

Similar to how the Renaissance in Italy emphasized a return to classicism, Latin at this time was used to purge the language of the changes made from Medieval Latin. People wished to return to the language that was used in the golden age of Latin literature during the Roman Empire. The humanists' efforts were successful in education, but ultimately, this wish to return to classicism would lead to the extinction of the language.

∽

Because humanists during the Renaissance were writing in an old language, they did not have the proper vocabulary for current issues. This gave the language an old, antiquated feel. Over time, less was written in Latin, until ultimately, the language became extinct. From that point on and to this day, the most common form of Latin is known as New Latin. This is Latin used for international scientific vocabulary, systematics, and the classification of species.

GREEK

Mycenaean Greek is the oldest form of the Greek language. It was spoken from the sixteenth to the eleventh century B.C.E. in Mycenae and Crete. The Linear B script tablets, which showed a system of writing based on a syllabic alphabet, is the only record of Mycenaean Greek. The language consisted of eighty-eight signs representing syllables and made no distinction between long and short vowels, or double consonants.

∽

Classical Greek, or Ancient Greek, was widely spoken throughout the Roman Empire, and it is the language found in the works of Homer and all of the famous Athenian philosophers. There were three distinctive forms and dialects of the language based on the different tribes and their locations: Dorian (the coast of Peloponnesus), Aeolian (the Aegean islands), and Ionian (the west coast of Asia Minor).

∽

Hellenistic Greek, or Koine Greek, is traced back to the Hellenistic colonization created by the conquests of Alexander the Great. It was the first common Greek dialect, and it was developed from a mixture of the Attic dialect (a subdialect of Ionic spoken in Athens) and other Greek dialects. It became the lingua franca across the Mediterranean, meaning the common language among people who spoke various languages. This was also the language used in the translation of the Christian New Testament.

∽

Medieval Greek, also known as Byzantine Greek, was spoken during the Byzantine Empire from 600 to the Ottoman conquest of Constantinople in 1453. It was the only language used in government and it is still the language used in the Greek Orthodox Church. Medieval Greek is considered to be the link between Ancient Greek and Modern Greek.

∽

Modern Greek refers to the language spoken from the fall of the Byzantine Empire in 1453 until now. There were two forms of the language spoken: Demotic and Katharevousa. Conceived in the early nineteenth century, Katharevousa was used for literature, scientific, administrative, and juridical purposes, and it was an imitation of the Classical Greek language. In 1976, Demotic was announced as the official language of Greece, and this is now known as Standard Modern Greek.

∽

Here are some helpful phrases to use when traveling in Greece:

- Hello (singular). *Yia sou.*
- Hello (plural). *Yia sas.*

- Thank you. *Efharisto.*
- Excuse me. *Signomi.*
- Please. *Parakalo.*
- Where is the toilet, please? *Pou ine i twaleta, parakalo?*
- Where is the beach? *Pou ine i paralia?*
- Sorry, I don't speak Greek. *Signomi, ala then milao elinika.*
- How much is it? *Poso kani?*

PORTUGUESE

Portuguese is the sixth most spoken language in the world. It is a Romance language that evolved from Latin, which was spoken on the western coast of the Iberian Peninsula. From 409 to 711 C.E., Germanic people inhabited the land, which led to regional variation. From the ninth to eleventh centuries, Portuguese-Galician was first being used in official administrative documents. In the eleventh century, the Christians of the region took over the land, and Portuguese and Galician split.

လ

There are many types of dialects found in Portuguese, but the two main ones can be broken down into Brazilian and European. The differences between the two involve different grammatical forms and phonology. The European dialect is more like that spoken by Portugal's former Asian and African colonies. The Brazilian dialect is primarily spoken in Brazil, and is the most common form.

လ

Portuguese is a West Iberian Romance language, and is closely related to Spanish, Galician, Fala, Leonese, and Mirandese. Galician and Fala are the closest languages to Portuguese. Galician and Portuguese used to be one language called Galician-Portuguese, and the vocabulary of Galician is still very similar to Portuguese. Fala is a descendant of Galician-Portuguese, and is spoken in several small towns in Spain.

ⓈⓈ

In 1990, an international treaty was made to unify the writing system of Portuguese that would be used by all Portuguese-speaking countries. The treaty made changes in the spelling of both European and Brazilian Portuguese. Some letters were removed, the letters *k*, *w*, and *y* were added to the Portuguese alphabet, and guidelines were made for the use of the hyphen and capitalization.

ⓈⓈ

Around 240 million people speak Portuguese today, and it is the official language of nine countries. Portuguese is the most widely spoken language of the Southern Hemisphere. Attempts have been made to turn Portuguese into an official language of the United Nations; however, it has faced several challenges, such as the fact that many Portuguese speakers all live on the same continent.

ⓈⓈ

Here are some helpful phrases to use when traveling to a Portuguese-speaking country:

- Hello. *Olá.*
- Goodbye. *Adeus.*
- Good day. *Bom dia.*
- Good evening. *Boa noite.*
- Yes. *Sim.*
- No. *Não.*
- Thank you. *Obrigado.*
- How much? *Quanto?*

- I don't speak Portuguese. *Eu não falo Português.*
- Hey, ref! Where's the penalty? *Oí, árbitro! Cadê o penalty?*
- Brazil is magnificent! *O Brasil é lindo maravilhoso!*

DUTCH

Dutch is a part of the West Germanic dialect, and more specifically, it is a West Low Franconian language. Dutch can be traced back to 500 C.E., when Old Frankish was split by the High German consonant shift. The Dutch language is broken down into periods: Old Dutch, which lasted from 500 to 1150; Middle Dutch, which lasted from 1150 to 1500; and Modern Dutch, which began in 1500 and is still spoken today.

∽

Dialects in Dutch are extremely diverse, and there is said to be about twenty-eight distinct dialects. *Flemish* is the term used for the type of Dutch spoken in Belgium, and in Flanders there are four types of Flemish: West Flemish, East Flemish, Brabantian, and Limburgish. Flemish is considered a softer dialect, and it favors older words. Netherlandish Dutch, in contrast, is considered to be harsh and even hostile sounding. In the east of the country, Dutch Low Saxon is spoken. Hollandic is one of the most common dialects in the Netherlands.

∽

Voiceless pronunciation with some letters—saying hard sounds instead of using one's voice—has started to become the standard for the language. This change mirrors a movement to make the spelling of Dutch words as phonological as possible. Another change that has not been declared an official change to the standard language, but has begun appearing in the younger generation, is known as Polder Dutch.

∽

Polder Dutch is a variation of Dutch spoken by the younger generation. In Polder Dutch (a term coined by Jan Stroop), diphthongs are pronounced with a wider mouth, and are pronounced lower. Polder Dutch seems to have begun around the 1970s, and originally it was middle-aged women and the upper-middle class who were pronouncing these diphthongs in this way. It has since spread.

∽

Dutch is currently the native language of Belgium, the Netherlands, and the Republic of Suriname. Dutch is said to be somewhere in between German and English; however, it most closely resembles German. It is spoken by 22 million people worldwide and was standardized in the seventeenth century. Dutch today sounds more like the dialect found in Holland.

EXTRACURRICULARS: STUDENT COUNCIL

Every U.S. President has spoken English as a first language except for one. Eighth president **MARTIN VAN BUREN**'s first language was Dutch, though he also spoke English.

∽

Here are helpful phrases when traveling in a Dutch-speaking country:

- Hello. *Hallo.*
- Good morning. *Goedemorgen.*
- Good afternoon. *Goedemiddag.*
- Good evening. *Goedenavond.*
- Have a nice day. *Nog een prettige dag.*
- Excuse me. *Neem me niet kwalijk.*

- How much is this? *Hoeveel kost dit?*
- Thank you. *Dank U.*
- Where's the toilet? *Waar is de WC?*
- Goodbye. *Tot ziens.*

JUNIOR YEAR: INTERMEDIATE LANGUAGES

RUSSIAN

In the sixth century, the Slav people migrated from Old Poland and gradually occupied the Balkans. By the tenth century, Western, Southern, and Eastern Slavonic had emerged as three similar, yet distinct, language groups. Eastern Slavonic is a direct ancestor of what would become Belarusian, Ukrainian, and Russian. The languages shared many grammatical rules and were able to share one written language (and only a written language), known as Old Slavonic.

∽

In the ninth century, Constantine and Methodius, two missionaries, were ordered to write down the language of Old Slavonic and preach to the people of Moravia about Christianity. Constantine, who on his deathbed changed his name to Cyril, created a Slavonic alphabet that is now known as Cyrillic. The Cyrillic alphabet was closely based on the Greek alphabet.

∽

In the early eighteenth century, Peter the Great came to power in Russia. With his political reforms came a reform of the alphabet that modified and simplified it and removed some of the Greek letters.

Some vocabulary from Western Europe was introduced, and the language reflected Post-Renaissance Europe instead of the Byzantine Empire's way of pronouncing words.

∽

By the middle of the eighteenth century, there was a need for the written Russian language to reflect the actual language spoken. Three distinct styles were distinguished: high style, also known as Church Slavonic, which was to be spoken for religion and poetics; middle style, which was used for science and prose; and low style, which was to be used for low comedies and personal correspondence. The middle style would come to form the Russian language that exists today. It was a combination of East Slavonic and Church Slavonic.

∽

Shortly after the Russian Revolution, and as a direct result of political ideology, the Russian language was simplified once again. This time, four letters were removed, and one silent letter used at the end of words was also removed. New political terminology was introduced, and the politeness characteristic of the upper classes was also removed. These steps were characteristic of what the new authoritarian regime set out to accomplish.

∽

Here are some helpful phrases to use when traveling to Russia. Note that these are not written with the Russian alphabet, but rather pronunciations that have been written in English:

- Good day. *Dobry den.*
- Hi/Hello. *Privet.*
- Do you speak English? *Govorite li vy po angliyski?*
- I need to use the restroom. *Mne nuzhno otoyti v tualet.*

- What time is it? *Kotoryy chas?*
- Goodbye. *Do svidaniya.*
- Yes. *Da.*
- No. *Net.*

EXTRACURRICULARS: YEARBOOK
MOST LIKELY TO УСПЕХА

Vladimir Nabokov was born in Russia and emigrated with his family to England after the Bolshevik Revolution. He lived in Germany, France, and then finally moved to the United States. He wrote the first of his novels in Russian, and the rest in English, including his best known, *Lolita*.

POLISH

Polish is a Western Slavonic language. During the Middle Ages, as the proto-Slavonic tribes settled in Europe, three groups emerged: West, East, and South. The Polish language began to emerge during the tenth century, when the first Polish state was established. As Christianity spread through the land, the Polish adopted the Latin alphabet, which allowed people for the first time to write Polish, a language that until then had only been spoken. Over time, additional letters were added.

∽

There are several dialects of Polish. Greater Polish is the dialect of the west, Lesser Polish is spoken in southern and southeastern Poland, Mazovian is spoken in eastern and central parts, Silesian is spoken in the south and southwest, and Highlander is spoken on the border of Poland and the Czech Republic and Slovakia. Highlander is strongly influenced by Romanian, as a result of migrants.

Kashubian is one of the more commonly spoken variants of Polish. It is spoken in the north of Poland, west of Gdansk, and in Pomerania. The argument over whether Kashubian is a distinct language on its own or another dialect of Polish has long been disputed. It has been decided that Kashubian is in fact another language; however, the similarities between the languages are striking. Nevertheless, those who speak Polish will not understand Kashubian unless it is written down.

Grammar in Polish is heavily influenced by the Old Slavic system of grammar. The endings of nouns, pronouns, and adjectives change according to function, with seven distinctions (nominative, genitive, dative, accusative, instrumental, locative, and vocative). There are also two number classes (singular and plural), and like many Slavic languages, there aren't any definite or indefinite articles.

There are 50 million Polish speakers worldwide. Polish is the official language of Poland; however, it is used as a secondary language in some parts of Lithuania, Russia, Belarus, Kazakhstan, and Ukraine. This is a result of migration, resettlements, and border changes from the Yalta Conference following World War II. Today, Polish is the third most widely spoken Slavic language.

Here are some helpful phrases to use when traveling in Poland:

- Good morning. *Dzień dobry.*
- Good evening. *Dobry wieczór.*
- Hello. *Cześć.*

- Goodbye. *Do widzenia* (formal)/*Do zobaczenia*/*Narazie!*/*Cześć!* (informal)
- I don't understand. *Nie rozumiem.*
- I speak English. *Mówię po angielsku.*
- Thank you. *Dzięki*/*Dziękuję*/*Serdecznie dziękuję.*
- Where is the toilet? *Gdzie jest toaleta?*
- How much is it? *Ile to kosztuje?*/*Po ile to jest?*

CZECH

Czech is a Western Slavonic language that was known as Bohemian until the nineteenth century. The earliest written documents in Czech date back to the eleventh century, and they were written in the Latin alphabet. Due to geographical location and a turbulent political history, the Czech language is greatly influenced by German and has grammatical and phonetic features of both German and Slavonic.

∽

In the fifteenth century, Jan Hus, a religious reformer, standardized the spelling of the language. In his reform, he attributed one letter to every sound. By adding certain accents (in the form of dots or lines) to certain letters, Hus was able to create a standard of spelling based on the Latin alphabet. This system is still in use to this day.

∽

Up until the fourteenth century, the Czech language was suppressed. It was considered to be a language spoken by peasants, not worthy of literature or any kind of standardization. For the first time, following the work of Jan Hus, Czech appeared in literature. In the nineteenth century, a movement to standardize the dialect to an older form of Czech took place. In Moravia and Silesia, this dialect is still spoken.

The Czech language and the Slovak language are very similar. The two countries were once a single country, Czechoslovakia. However, when the Communist regime fell, they broke apart, becoming the Czech Republic and Slovakia. Though there are slight differences, speakers of Czech can understand and read Slovak, and vice versa.

Two major dialects can be found in the Czech language relating to geographic location. The most commonly used dialect is called Common Czech, which is used around Bohemia. The other dialect pertains to Moravia and Silesia, which is based on standard Czech. Moravia and Silesia have more localized dialects than Common Czech. In Silesia, for example, there exists a community that speaks a combination of Czech and Polish.

Here are some helpful phrases to use when traveling to the Czech Republic:

- Hello. *Dobrý den.*
- Good morning. *Dobré ráno.*
- Good evening. *Dobrý večer.*
- What's your name? *Jak se jmenujete?*
- I don't speak Czech. *Nemluvím česky.*
- I don't understand. *Nerozumím.*
- Thank you. *Děkuji.*
- Where is the bathroom? *Kde jsou toalety?*
- How much is this? *Kolik to stojí?*
- Goodbye. *Na shledanou.*

HEBREW

Hebrew is a Semitic language, and a member of the Afro-Asiatic family. According to Judaism, Hebrew was the first language. Hebrew is a Northwest Semitic language which began around the third century B.C.E. The first written evidence of the language is from around the tenth century B.C.E., and this is what is referred to as Classic Hebrew. Around 1,700 years ago, the spoken language was displaced by Aramaic, though it remained a written language. Not until the nineteenth century was the spoken language revived.

ဟ

From the fourth century to the nineteenth century, Hebrew existed solely as a written language. In 1881, Eliezer Ben-Yehuda revived Hebrew as a spoken language based on the liturgical language.

ဟ

In the 1880s, three types of Hebrew accents existed: Sephardi (Hispanic and Mediterranean), Ashkenazi (German), and that of Jews that were separate from both, living in Iraq, Yemen, Morocco, and Tunisia. The standard Hebrew that Eliezer Ben-Yehuda created was supposed to be based on Sephardi pronunciation and Mishnaic spelling. However, for many of the earliest speakers, Yiddish was their native tongue, and so idioms and literal translations were brought into the language from Yiddish. Instead of Sephardi phonology, the Ashkenazi style was used.

ဟ

The Hebrew language has existed for over 2,000 years and little of the language has changed. Because of this fact, the language is deeply rooted in the Jewish religion, used for prayer and study, and the Torah, the Jewish Bible, is written in Hebrew. Ashkenazi, Sephardi, and Mizrahi relate to the different pronunciations of the language, and though Modern Hebrew is established, all of these pronunciations are still used in religious ceremonies and rituals.

∽

The Hebrew alphabet, which is written from right to left, is an abjad. It consists of twenty-two letters, all consonants. The script is a square script, and it is based on Aramaic script (or Ashurit). There is also a cursive version of the alphabet for writing. If vowels are necessary, diacritic marks are placed above or below the letters and sometimes consonants are used as vowels.

∽

Here are some helpful Hebrew phrases to use when traveling to Israel (or maybe attending a service). Note that these are written phonetically:

- Hello. *Shalom.*
- Good morning. *Boker tov.*
- Good afternoon. *Achar tzahara'im tovim.*
- Good evening. *Erev tov.*
- Pleased to meet you. *Na'im me'od.*
- I don't understand. *Ani lo mevin* (when said by a man); *Ani lo mevinah* (when said by a woman).
- How much is this? *Kama ze ole?*
- Thank you. *Rav todot.*
- Where's the toilet? *Eifo ha'sheirutim?*
- Goodbye. *Lehitraot.*

SENIOR YEAR: ADVANCED LANGUAGES

JAPANESE

Japanese is a Japonic language, and is related to Altaic and Ryuky-uan languages. The Japanese language has gone through four distinct phases, known as Old Japanese (which ended around the eighth century C.E., a period that saw the beginning of significant influence from Chinese); Early Middle Japanese (from 794 to 1185); Late Middle Japanese (from 1185 to 1600, where European languages began influencing the language); and Modern Japanese (from 1600 to today).

ဟ

The Japanese writing system of today is a blend of the Chinese writing system, two kana syllabaries (alphabets based on symbols developed during the ninth century to simplify writing), and Roman numerals and letters. From the third to the fifth century, Japanese used Classical Chinese as the official writing system. As the language evolved, several distinct differences separated the Japanese form of writing from the Chinese. One notable difference is that Chinese is a monosyllabic language (all words are one syllable), and Japanese is polysyllabic.

ဟ

The Japanese language does not have any diphthongs. Instead, it is composed of monophthongs, meaning the vowels in the language are pure. There are five vowels in Japanese, *a*, *i*, *u*, *o*, and *e*, and each has a long and short form. Most of the syllables in Japanese end with a vowel sound. Japanese has a pitched accent, meaning pitch falls following the syllable that is accented.

There is a very complex system in the Japanese language when dealing with the issue of politeness, and at least four different levels of how to address a person. How to address someone is based on a variety of factors such as age, job, and experience, and there is even a different form of politeness when asking someone for a favor. There are differences between the polite language, *teineigo*, the respectful language, *sonkeigo*, and the humble language, *kenjōgo*, as well as differences between honorific and humble forms.

§

Due to the mountainous terrain and a history of internal and external isolation, there are many dialects of Japanese. These differ in vocabulary, pitch accent, morphology of certain types of words, and sometimes pronunciation. Though there are dozens of dialects, they can be broken into two main categories: Eastern and Western. Eastern dialects emphasize the sounds of consonants more, and the Western dialects emphasize vowels more.

§

Here are some useful phrases to use when traveling in Japan. Note, these are spelled out phonetically:

- How are you? *O genki desu ka?*
- Pleased to meet you. *Hajimemashite.*
- Good morning. *Ohayō gozaimasu.*
- Good evening. *Konbanwa.*
- Excuse me. *Sumimasen.*
- How much is this? *Ikura desu ka?*
- Thank you. *Arigato.*
- Where's the toilet? *Benjo wa doko desu ka?*
- Goodbye. *Sayōnara.*

MANDARIN

There are many variations in the Chinese language. Mandarin is spoken in southwestern and northern China and is a Sino-Tibetan language. It began as the language of the courts starting in the Ming Dynasty, with the dialect of Beijing being very influential. By the seventeenth century, schools were set up to teach the Beijing style, and this dialect was established as the national language in 1909. The Beijing style continued to be the national language when the Republic of China came to power and there was a greater need for a common language.

§

From 960 to 1127 B.C.E., Emperor Taizu of the Northern Song Dynasty conquered the lands that we now know as China. When the Northern Song Dynasty came to an end, what is referred to as Old Mandarin, a new common speech, developed. Literature and art flourished during this time, and were written in this vernacular form. Much of the grammatical elements, rules, and syntax are retained in the Mandarin spoken today.

§

Even when the Qing Dynasty fell and the Republic of China came to power, Mandarin remained the official language. When the People's Republic of China came to power in 1949, the effort to make Mandarin the national language continued, and the Beijing dialect became the official language, now known as Standard Chinese. Mandarin is the official language used in the media and in education. Though Taiwan and some of mainland China (such as Hong Kong) still speak Cantonese, Mandarin is spoken fluently as well. Officially, there are two types of Mandarin, one that the PRC government refers to, and one that the ROC government refers to.

§

Mandarin is known as a stress-timed language. What this means is that syllables, as in English, can last for different lengths of time, but there is still a constant amount of time between the stressed syllables. Mandarin differs from other Chinese languages such as Cantonese and Min Nan for this very reason. Cantonese and Min Nan are known as syllable-timed languages, where each syllable takes the same amount of time.

§

Mandarin is one of the most widely spoken languages in the world, and due to China's size and population, there are many Mandarin dialects spoken. The dialects include the Northeastern dialect, the Southwestern dialect, the Beijing dialect (which Standard Chinese is based on), the Zhongyuan dialect, and the Jilu dialect. Almost all the cities in China have their own variation on Mandarin.

§

Here are some useful phrases to use when traveling to China. Note that these are written in pinyin, which is a phonetic spelling that uses the Latin alphabet (with the inclusion of *zh*, *ch*, *sh*, and no *v*):

- Hello. *Nǐ hǎo.*
- Good morning. *Zǎoān.*
- Good afternoon. *Wǔān.*
- Good evening. *Wǎnān.*
- I don't understand. *Wǒ tīngbùdǒng.*
- Excuse me. *Duìbùqǐ.*
- Where's the toilet? *Cèsuǒ zài nǎli?*
- How much is this? *Zhège duōshǎo qián?*
- Goodbye. *Zàijiàn.*

CANTONESE

Cantonese originated in southern China. It is the most prestigious dialect of the Yue language. It is believed to have formed following the fall of the Han Dynasty in 220 C.E., due to isolation. By the Tang Dynasty in 618 C.E., Cantonese was its own distinct dialect. Because Hong Kong was a British colony from the mid-nineteenth century to the late twentieth century, it was shielded from many of the linguistic reforms of China, most notably, the shift to Mandarin as the standard language.

*

Though both Cantonese and Mandarin share the same basic alphabet, the two languages have very distinct sounds when spoken. Cantonese is thought to be more complex than Mandarin, with up to nine tones compared to Mandarin's four. The most obvious difference is the location of people who speak these languages. Whereas Mandarin is used in mainland China and Taiwan, Cantonese is spoken in southern China. It is said that when comparing the two, it is like having a duck try to talk to a chicken. Though they are both birds, the species are very different.

*

Cantonese literature is more developed than any other Chinese language. Though the writing system uses the same characters as the standard language, it also has additional characters, and some characters even have different meanings. There are also words in Cantonese that do not have any meaning in Mandarin. Instead of a new or different written language, Cantonese is written in the same system as Mandarin, and the words are just pronounced differently.

⌁

The pronunciation of Cantonese is based on the language spoken in the capital of the Guangdong Province, Canton. In the Cantonese syllabary, there are around 630 sounds and 1,760 syllables. The nine different tones have different meanings when combined with syllables. From a phonological standpoint, Cantonese is a much more difficult language to understand than Mandarin.

⌁

A total of 71 million people speak Cantonese, and it is spoken in Hong Kong, Guangdong, Macau, Hainan, and Guangxi. Through Western colonialism, migration, and trade, the majority of Chinese who have traveled abroad have been speakers of Cantonese. Today, Cantonese-speaking communities appear more in other countries than in most of China. The United States and Canada have the most Cantonese-speaking communities outside of Hong Kong and mainland China, and in San Francisco, there are a total of 180,000 Cantonese speakers.

⌁

Here are some helpful phrases to use when traveling to Hong Kong. Note that these are written in Yale Romanization, a phonetic English alphabet:

- Pleased to meet you. *Hóu hòisàm yihngsīk néih.*
- Good morning. *Jóusàhn.*
- Good day. *Ńgh ōn.*
- Good evening. *Máahn ōn.*
- Excuse me. *m̀hgòi.*
- How much is this? *Nīgo géidō chín a?*
- Thank you. *Dòjeh.*
- Where's the toilet? *Chisó hái bīndouh a?*

- Do you speak English? *Neih sīkm̀hsīk góng yìngmán a?*
- Can you translate it for me? *Néih hóm̀hhóyíh bòng ngóh fáanyihk a?*
- Goodbye. *Joigin.*

KOREAN

The Korean language is a Ural-Altaic language. Ural-Altaic languages originated in northern Asia and include the Turkic, Mongol, Finnish, Hungarian, and Manchu languages. Despite grammatical similarities, a relationship between Korean and Japanese has not been discovered yet. From 108 B.C.E. to 313 C.E., the Chinese occupied northern Korea, and by the fifth century, Classical Chinese was the written language and much of the Chinese language was borrowed.

∽

The Korean alphabet, Hangul, was created in 1444. The consonants got their shape based on the shape the mouth made when the sound was pronounced. The writing direction (vertically and right to left) and method of writing the symbols in blocks was taken from the Chinese. After Hangul was created, most Koreans could write in both Hangul and Classical Chinese, and during the nineteenth and twentieth centuries, a mix of the two systems (Hanja) became popular until 1945 when use of Chinese characters diminished.

∽

The vocabulary of the Korean language is a blend of pure Korean words and Sino-Korean words, which were taken from written Chinese or Korean words in Chinese characters. This is similar to how Indo-European languages infused Greek and Latin into their languages. Today, many of the loanwords found in the language are from the English language. The vocabulary of North Korea favors the native Korean vocabulary over the Sino-Korean vocabulary.

There are many dialects found in Korean. In South Korea, the standard language is based on the dialect of Seoul. In North Korea, the standard language is based on the dialect of Pyongyang. The dialects found in both North Korea and South Korea are mutually intelligible. The dialect that is most noticeably different is that of Jeju Island, which features many archaic words that have since been lost in the Korean language of today.

Though North Korea and South Korea speak the same language, the lasting separation from each other has created subtle differences in the languages. While they both use the same letters, called jamo, some of the letters have different names. Also, the North uses a different stroke in one jamo than the South, and compound vowel and tense consonant jamos are not treated separately in South Korea but are in North Korea, and some jamos have different names.

Here are some helpful phrases to use when traveling to Korea. Note that these are written out phonetically:

- Hello. *Annyeonghaseyo.*
- How are you? *Eotteohke jinaeseyo?*
- Pleased to meet you. *Mannaseo bangapseumnida.*
- Good morning/afternoon/evening. *Annyeong hashimnikka.*
- I don't understand. *Moreugesseumnida.*
- How much is this? *Ige eolmayeyo?*
- Thank you. *Kamsahamnida.*
- Where's the toilet? *Hwajangsiri eodiyeyo.*
- Excuse me. *Shillehagessumnida.*
- Goodbye. *Annyeonghi gyeseyo.*

PERIOD 9
ART

STUDIES HAVE SHOWN THAT ART EDU-CATION BENEFITS overall achievement, so let's not forget to include an elective in your schedule. Having a base level knowledge of the arts makes any trip to a museum a little more interesting, and gives every song you hear on the radio a little more zip. And plus, a well-timed tidbit about Baroque realism, an obscure fact about Picasso, or knowledge of cool jazz will always impress your friends at any dinner party.

FRESHMAN YEAR: INTRODUCTION TO ART HISTORY

ANCIENT GREEK ART

The art of ancient Greece placed great attention on mimicking nature and understanding the human figure.

∽

The **ARCHAIC** period lasted from 750 to 500 B.C.E., and was heavily influenced by the large sculptures of Egypt. The art focused on accurately portraying the human figure, steering away from human patterning.

∽

In the **CLASSICAL** period (480–338 B.C.E.), human figures became freestanding and were sculpted in stone and bronze. Statues portrayed gods as perfect humans.

∽

This was the first period when individual sculptors became known for their work. One example is **PHIDIAS**, a sculptor who also is known to have overseen the construction of the Parthenon.

∽

HELLENISTIC art (338–331 B.C.E.) shifted away from religion and more toward naturalism, realism, and human psychology.

∽

During this period, instead of the idea of the perfect human, emphasis was put on everyday people and their imperfections, including expressions of pain and despair.

BYZANTINE ART

When the Roman Empire fell, the Eastern Roman Empire continued to flourish. Over time this became known as the **BYZANTINE EMPIRE**.

∽

Artwork of the Byzantine Empire was greatly influenced by the art of ancient Greece and incorporated many of its themes.

∽

The humanism found in Greek art was replaced with the ideals of Orthodox Christianity.

∽

Byzantine art focused on religion and less attention was paid to realism.

∽

The artwork also introduced iconography and symbols painting.

∽

Byzantine paintings depicted God, Jesus, the Virgin Mary, and saints.

RENAISSANCE ART

The **RENAISSANCE** marked the rebirth of ancient Greek principles in art after the Middle Ages.

∽

In the **EARLY RENAISSANCE** (1330–1450), artwork was focused again on humanism and naturalism. To attain realism, artists incorporated depth of field, linear perspective, and new methods of shading.

DONATELLO's sculptures of David, the first in marble, and the second cast in bronze, depict the naked youth standing over the head of Goliath and are good example of works from the period.

During the **HIGH RENAISSANCE** (1490–1530), the techniques that began earlier were being mastered by artists.

LEONARDO DA VINCI, **MICHELANGELO**, and **RAPHAEL** are all artists of the time. Michelangelo's famous sculpture *David* is an example of a work coming out of this period.

The principles of the Italian Renaissance spread through Europe leading to the **NORTHERN RENAISSANCE** (1500–1600).

Jan van Eyck's *The Arnolfini Portrait* is an example of art from this period, which presented everyday scenes with common people.

BAROQUE ART

Starting in Italy, **BAROQUE** paintings, sculptures, and architecture reflected the religious tension between the Catholic Church and the Protestant Reformation.

Baroque art in Catholic areas consisted of large paintings and frescos in order to attract the most viewers.

Departing from the style of Renaissance art, where the human form was idealized, Baroque paintings portrayed people realistically.

ဟ

FAMOUS BAROQUE ARTISTS:

- **CARAVAGGIO:** *David and Goliath* depicts David as he stands over the giant he has just taken down. The scene illuminates the two realistic characters so that much of their bodies are hidden in the shadows.
- **REMBRANDT:** *The Storm on the Sea of Galilee*, the only seascape by the artist, depicts the apostles in the rough sea praying for help from Jesus.

EXTRACURRICULARS: DRAMA CLUB

Many actors have played artists in films. **KIRK DOUGLAS** played Vincent van Gogh, **SALMA HAYEK** played Frida Kahlo, **ED HARRIS** played Jackson Pollack, **JEFFREY WRIGHT** played Jean-Michel Basquiat, and **CHARLTON HESTON** played Michelangelo.

SOPHOMORE YEAR: ADVANCED ART HISTORY

IMPRESSIONISM

Starting in France around 1867, **IMPRESSIONISM** was one of the first major shifts away from the traditions of painting.

Artists placed more emphasis on color and light and less on form, often featuring loose brushstrokes and bright colors.

∽

Many artists would paint outside for a day, capturing a brief snapshot of the light. The result was an in-depth study of light and color.

∽

The name of the movement comes from an art critic who described Claude Monet's *Impression, Sunrise* as not being finished, and just an impression of a painting.

∽

FAMOUS IMPRESSIONIST WORKS:

- *Water Lilies* by Claude Monet
- *A Bar at the Folies-Bergère* by Édouard Manet
- *Bal du moulin de la Galette* by Pierre-Auguste Renoir

EXPRESSIONISM

EXPRESSIONISM (1905–1925) was the opposite of Impressionism. Expressionists attempted to express the emotions, often extreme and distorted, of the artist or subject. The movement is mostly known for work produced out of Germany after World War I.

∽

Expressionism placed importance on color and line to express emotions.

Among the greatest influences of Expressionism were the later works of **VINCENT VAN GOGH**.

✺

FAMOUS EXPRESSIONIST WORKS:

- *The Funeral* by George Grosz
- *The Scream* by Edvard Munch
- *Portrait of Dr. Heinrich Stadelmann* by Otto Dix

CUBISM

CUBISM (1907–1914) began in Paris as a response to break away from Impressionism. It broke down objects into their more simple geometric shapes while also depicting different viewpoints.

✺

Cubism was heavily influenced by the works of **PAUL CÉZANNE**, and lead by **PABLO PICASSO** and **GEORGES BRAQUE**.

✺

HERMETIC CUBISM broke down the image even more to the point that the subject of the painting was unrecognizable.

✺

SYNTHETIC CUBISM combined high and low art by incorporating the use of collages of found objects like newspapers and painting.

FAMOUS CUBIST WORKS:

- *Woman with a Mandolin* by Pablo Picasso
- *Guernica* by Pablo Picasso
- *Violin and Candlestick* by Georges Braque

EXTRACURRICULARS: STUDENT COUNCIL

Since finishing up his presidency in 2009, George W. Bush has taken up painting. His art has been on display at his presidential library in Dallas.

DADAISM

Originating in Zurich, Switzerland, **DADAISM** (1916–1923) was formed by artists, writers, and intellectuals in response to World War I. Their reaction to the war was one of disgust and protest, and they classified their works as **ANTI-ART**.

The one rule of Dadaism was: don't follow the rules of art.

The works were meant to shock and elicit emotional reactions.

FAMOUS IMPRESSIONIST ARTISTS:

- Marcel Duchamp
- Jean Arp
- George Grosz

JUNIOR YEAR: MODERN ART

SURREALISM

SURREALISM, or the art of the subconscious began in 1924. It stemmed from Dadaism, and was founded by André Breton.

∽

Surrealism was heavily influenced by the works of Sigmund Freud and Carl Jung.

∽

The work focused on eliciting a response from the subconscious.

∽

Instead of displaying what was seen in the world like that of traditional artwork, surrealists created impossible landscapes and imagery in an attempt to open the mind and capture the human psyche.

∽

SALVADOR DALÍ is the most famous of the surrealists.

∽

FAMOUS SURREALIST WORKS:

- *The Persistence of Memory* by Salvador Dalí
- *The Son of Man* by René Magritte
- *The Elephant Celebes* by Max Ernst

POP ART

POP ART (1955–1970) started in England and eventually moved to the United States and was in response to abstract impressionism and elitism it produced.

ᴄᴏ

Pop art used ideas and themes from popular culture like films, celebrities, advertisements, and television, and focused on contemporary issues.

ᴄᴏ

Pop art was more understandable and related to a broader population, in particular, the youth of the 1950s and 1960s.

ᴄᴏ

Pop art set out to show that art could be made out of nontraditional mediums, that the concept was more important than the physical piece of art, and rejected the notion of high art.

ᴄᴏ

ANDY WARHOL is the best-known and most influential pop artist.

ᴄᴏ

Warhol dealt with familiar icons such as Campbell's Soup and Marilyn Monroe, but in different mediums, including paint, silkscreen, film, drawing, and photography.

ᴄᴏ

ROY LICHTENSTEIN and **JASPER JOHNS** were two other prominent and popular pop artists.

CONTEMPORARY ART MOVEMENTS

CONTEMPORARY ART is the art of today, spanning roughly from 1960 to the present.

§

Since the movements are ongoing, they are not as carefully defined yet as the previous movements.

§

NEO-POP was the renewed interest in pop art that grew in the 1980s.

§

Neo-Pop was similar to the original pop artists, in that in evaluated obsessions in Western culture. Jeff Koons's sculpture *Michael Jackson and Bubbles* is one example.

§

In 1999, the **STUCKISM** movement was founded to promote figurative painting and stray away from conceptual art. Paul Harvey is a one member of this group.

EXTRACURRICULARS: NEWSPAPER
FRANCIS BACON PAINTING MOST EXPENSIVE OF ALL TIME

In 2013, Francis Bacon's *Three Studies of Lucian Freud*, believed to be his defining work, came on to auction at Christie's, and sold for $142.4 million. To date this is the most ever spent on a work of art at auction. The painting, which consists of three panels, was completed in 1969.

∽

PHOTOREALISM is a movement that began in the 1960s using cameras to gain information, and then replicating the pictures with paint. Chuck Close is a prominent photorealist.

∽

Begun in 1992, **TOYISM** paintings are colorful, have a narrative, and appear humorous in nature, but deal with real human emotions.

∽

A Toyist example is *Live with Energy* by Srylyn.

SENIOR YEAR: MUSIC APPRECIATION

MUSIC TERMS

MUSIC is a form of art whose medium is sound. The basics of music are pitch, rhythm, dynamics, and timbre or texture.

∽

PITCH is basically how high or low a sound or note is. Pitch is determined by the speed of a sound's vibrations: the faster a note vibrates, the higher the pitch, and vice versa. In general, smaller objects vibrate faster and produce a higher pitch.

∽

A sound that has a definite pitch is called a **TONE**. The distance (measured in what are called **STEPS**) between any two tones is called an interval. When tones are eight steps or an octave apart, they sound very much alike. The lower tone in an octave vibrates half as fast as the higher tone. In early music, pitch was the only thing at the composer's disposal.

ϲⱺ

DYNAMICS is the difference between loudness and softness in music. **LOUDNESS** is related to how hard something is vibrating. Utilizing changes in dynamics offers composers different moods for their compositions. These changes can be made abruptly, gradually, or with a sense of rising or falling.

ϲⱺ

RHYTHM can be understood as how music flows over time. It's defined as the particular arrangement of note lengths in a piece of music. Rhythm is measured with a meter and based on a beat, or a regular occurring pulse to music.

ϲⱺ

Another part of rhythm is **TEMPO**, which is how fast the song is played. Tempo is marked as follows:

- *largo*: very slow, broad
- *grave*: very slow, solemn
- *adagio*: slow
- *andante*: moderately slow
- *moderato*: moderate
- *allegretto*: moderately fast
- *allegro*: fast
- *vivace*: lively
- *presto*: very fast
- *prestissimo*: as fast as possible

∽

TIMBRE is the property of a musical sound that describes how the tone resonates. It can be dark, light, airy, hard, mellow, or anywhere in between. Different instruments have different tone colors; thus, a composer can use the same melody but play it on different instruments and keep the piece of music interesting.

CLASSICAL MUSIC

The **CLASSICAL ERA** (1750–1820) went from the complicated, polyphonic, and hard-to-play-and-sing music of Baroque, to a simpler, easier-to-sing-and-remember style that we all know as classical.

∽

By 1770 the classical style was fully developed with the works of Joseph Haydn, Wolfgang Amadeus Mozart, and Ludwig van Beethoven. By the time classical music really caught on, music had become a commodity for the masses. Thus composers started writing simpler music that amateur musicians could play.

∽

The **SONATA** is a form for a single movement of a symphony or other composition usually used for the first part of a piece. It has three sections: the exposition that introduces a theme, the development where the themes are played by different instruments or in other various ways, and the recapitulation where the themes return.

∽

The **MINUET**, usually used as a third movement, was originally a stately dance song with curtsies and bows. However, the minuet form that is used in symphonies are for listening, not dancing, and is written in triple (¾) meter.

∽

The biggest contribution to music made in the classical era was the development of the **SYMPHONY**, a long piece that usually lasts between twenty and forty-five minutes. A symphony usually contains four movements, each of which has a different emotion. A theme that is introduced earlier in a piece will rarely appear in later movements.

∽

A **CONCERTO** is a three-movement composition made for an instrumental soloist and an orchestra. The soloist is the star of this composition and needs to be very talented in order to play this type of music. The concerto's tempo changes from fast to slow and back to fast. Prior to the nineteenth century, there was usually a complete, unaccompanied, improvised showcase by the soloist during the first movement and sometimes again in the third. But improvisation went into decline after the eighteenth century, and composers started writing down the solos.

∽

LUDWIG VAN BEETHOVEN: Many consider the works of Ludwig van Beethoven (1770–1827) to be the highest form of musical genius. Beethoven was considered a rebel; he thought an artist deserved as much respect as nobility. When Beethoven was twenty-nine, he noticed the first symptoms of deafness and suffered an emotional crisis afterward. His works following this crisis show new power and heroism. By 1818 Beethoven was completely deaf, and he stopped playing piano and conducting. Luckily, he didn't stop composing, and he wrote many piano sonatas, string quartets, and the renowned Ninth Symphony, all while totally deaf.

JAZZ

JAZZ started as a blend of various cultural musicalities, including West African, American, and European. Jazz is heavily influenced by West African drumming, improvisation, and intricate rhythms.

∽

A **JAZZ ENSEMBLE** is made up of a rhythm section consisting of a piano, plucked double bass, percussion, and occasionally guitars or banjos, and melodic instruments like the cornet, trumpet, saxophone, piano, clarinet, vibraphone, and trombone. The percussion uses the drum set, invented in the late 1800s, which has a snare drum, cymbals, and a bass drum operated by a foot pedal. Jazz solo musicians utilize brass, woodwinds, and percussions rather than the bowed strings of classical music.

∽

TYPES OF JAZZ:

- **NEW ORLEANS-STYLE JAZZ:** New Orleans was the center of jazz from 1900 to 1917. The city was home to many jazz artists, including Ferdinand "Jelly Roll" Morton, Joseph Nathan "King" Oliver, and Louis "Satchmo" Armstrong. New Orleans jazz was based on marches, church songs, or twelve-bar blues. Over time, soloists began to improvise new melodies based on the harmony of the song rather than the original melody of the song. By the 1920s, the trumpet replaced the cornet, and the saxophone was added.
- **SWING:** During the 1920s, a new style of jazz called swing sprung up. It flourished between 1935 and 1945, a decade that was later nicknamed the "swing era." Swing was played mainly by big bands, such as those led by Duke Ellington, Count Basie, and Benny Goodman. These bands featured instrumentalists and

occasionally singers such as Billie Holiday, Ella Fitzgerald, and Frank Sinatra.

- **BEBOP:** Bebop was a complex type of jazz meant for listening and not dancing. It had sophisticated harmonies and unpredictable rhythms that were bewildering to people accustomed to the regulated music of swing. Bebop performers were part of an exclusive group of musicians who weeded out other jazz musicians by using strange chord progressions and complex melodies. Bebop performers also used a "hip" language and dressed a special "hip" way with goatees and berets.

- **COOL JAZZ:** By the early 1950s, jazz had started to become calmer and more relaxed, thus the name cool jazz. The movement, led by Lester Young, Stan Getz, Lennie Tristano, and Miles Davis, featured a subdued kind of music that used a gentler approach. Instruments that were not previously used in jazz, such as the French horn, flute, and cello, started to make their appearance. Also, classical works such as those by Bach influenced some groups.

ᏕᏅ

IMPORTANT JAZZ ARTISTS:

- **DUKE ELLINGTON:** Edward Kennedy "Duke" Ellington (1899–1974) was a composer, arranger, and conductor, and is considered one of the most important players in the swing era. Even beyond that, he is widely held to be one of the most influential figures in the history of jazz. He wrote hundreds of three-minute pieces of music for his band and others, as well as for films, television, ballet, theater, and church.

- **CHARLIE "BIRD" PARKER:** Charlie Parker (1920–1955) was an alto saxophonist of impressive skill. He was a leading musician during the bebop era, and is still considered one of the best jazz improvisers of all time.

- **MILES DAVIS:** Miles Davis (1926–1991) was one of the most important players in jazz history. He was a leading figure in both cool jazz and the fusion style of jazz that mixed jazz and rock and roll.

ROCK AND ROLL

Rock and roll emerged in the 1940s from blues, rockabilly, jazz, and gospel music. Its instruments included a guitar (either electric or acoustic), a piano, an upright bass, a drum set, and a vocalist.

ഗ

Early artists included Elvis Presley, Buddy Holly, Chuck Berry, and Jerry Lee Lewis, most of whom were heavily influenced by the blues.

ഗ

By the 1960s, British rock bands started gaining popularity and made their way to American charts. These bands brought the English genre of skiffle to the mix. Their arrival was known as the **BRITISH INVASION,** which lasted from 1964 to 1966 and included the Rolling Stones, the Beatles, and the Who.

ഗ

HARD ROCK grew out of the late 1960s when blues rock bands such as Led Zeppelin and Deep Purple started playing heavier music that veered away from the blues format. By the early 1970s, hard rock had become distinctly different from blues rock, and the prime example of this was Led Zeppelin's album *Led Zeppelin II*. Hard rock continued to use the same instrumentation as blues rock but was played with more distortion and an even more driving beat. By the 1980s hard rock had evolved into a new genre called heavy metal. By the 1990s hard rock had turned into alternative rock, which included genres such as grunge.

PUNK ROCK evolved as an antithesis to the glamour and glitz that was associated with mainstream rock. It was created in the mid-1970s, and by 1976 it was crystallized in the United States in the form of the Ramones and in the United Kingdom with the Sex Pistols and the Clash. Punk rejected all the flair of the rock musicians, including the solos, the giant stages, the pyrotechnics, and the elaborate costumes.

ഗ

IMPORTANT ROCK ARTISTS:

- **THE BEATLES:** Rooted as much in British skiffle as in American rock and roll, the Beatles had an all-new sound. They debuted with "Please Please Me" in 1963, which landed at number one on the pops charts and led to a craze known as Beatlemania. The Beatles continued their stranglehold on the music industry even as their style evolved from a straightforward pop sound to more sophisticated folk, psychedelic, and blues influenced sound. The Beatles released their last album, *Abbey Road*, in 1969, and started to show signs of breaking up. By 1970 the Beatles were effectively over, but their influence on music is still felt today.
- **JIMI HENDRIX:** Jimi Hendrix (1942–1970) is considered the single most influential guitarist of all time due to his innovative use of feedback, distortion, and various other effects. His playing also reinvigorated the blues and laid the groundwork for heavy metal. Hendrix took the British rock scene by storm, blowing other guitarists out of the water with his blazing licks, and changed everyone's conception of how blues could be played. Hendrix released his first album *Are You Experienced* in 1967, which brought them new levels of fame.
- **NIRVANA:** Nirvana was formed in 1987 and signaled the beginning of alternative music's breaking through into the mainstream. Founded by Kurt Cobain and Krist Novoselic, Nirvana started

the grunge music trend, which was like punk rock but with more angst and played at a slower pace. Cobain's use of feedback and his bare bones style of guitar playing also influenced the next wave of hard and alternative rockers.

EXTRACURRICULARS: YEARBOOK
MOST LIKELY TO BECOME THE NEXT SUPERSTAR

AMERICAN IDOL took television and the music industry by storm in the summer of 2002, and crowned **KELLY CLARKSON**, who has arguably become its biggest star, the first winner. Since then the show has produced countless number-one singles, albums, and was the top show for the majority of its run.

PERIOD 10
SOCIAL
SCIENCE

THE SOCIAL SCIENCES ARE A GROUP OF ACADEMIC DISCIPLINES that apply scientific methods to the social relations of humans. Many of these studies had their roots in a desire for social betterment of society but now employ quantitative methods and statistics in their analysis of theories and trends. Use this information to find betterment in your own life, or just use it to perform experiments on your family and friends.

FRESHMAN YEAR: PSYCHOLOGY

INTRODUCTION TO PSYCHOLOGY

PSYCHOLOGY is a scientific approach to understanding the thought processes and behaviors of humans in their interaction with the environment.

∽

Psychologists study the processes of thinking and cognition, sense perception, learning, emotions and motivation, personality, abnormal behavior, and interactions between individuals and the environment.

∽

It is generally agreed that **WILHELM WUNDT** (1832–1920) founded psychology in 1879 when he established the first psychological laboratory at the University of Leipzig in Germany. Wundt set out to study the human mind using a method called **INTROSPECTION**.

∽

Introspection was also the approach used by William James (1842–1910) in the United States, when he wrote *The Principles of Psychology* (1890), which for most psychologists marked the beginning of modern psychology.

PSYCHOLOGY DISCIPLINES

BEHAVIORISM is a school of psychology that attempts to explain behavior in terms of observable and measurable responses to environmental stimuli. Biological processes are only reactions, and behaviorism discards such concepts as consciousness, ideas, and emotions.

ဪ

The conditioned-response experiments of Russian Ivan Pavlov and American Edward Thorndike were influential in the development of behaviorism. Behaviorist thought has led to behavior modification therapies employing conditioning, desensitization, and modeling.

ဪ

COGNITIVE PSYCHOLOGY studies human internal mental processes such as problem solving, memory, and language, particularly as they affect learning and behavior.

ဪ

Cognitive psychology took off in the 1960s, launched by the information-processing model developed by **ALLEN NEWELL** (1927–1992) and **HERBERT SIMON** (1916–2001) some years earlier. This model studies the similarities between the human brain and the computer in the ways information is received, processed, stored, and retrieved.

ဪ

HUMANIST PSYCHOLOGISTS, in reaction to the mainstream trends of behaviorism and psychoanalysis, argue that humans are individuals and should be treated as unique beings.

ဪ

Humanists hold that, although we certainly have needs in common with other animals and can be quite selfish at times, there's more to being human. We have goals in life, we have a need to grow and fulfill ourselves psychologically and feel good about it all, and we have a need to find happiness that goes beyond the satisfaction of basic needs. To the humanists, the positive thinking and hope that psychoanalysts and strict behaviorists ignored are the most important aspects of human behavior.

∽

BIOLOGICAL PSYCHOLOGY is the study of physiological bases of behavior, or the mind-body phenomenon.

∽

Biological psychology is being applied to areas such as understanding the physiological bases for learning and memory, emotionality, and mental and behavioral disorders.

SIGMUND FREUD

SIGMUND FREUD (1856–1939) developed his psychoanalytic theory in Austria over forty years.

∽

The prevailing view in the late nineteenth century was that humans are rational beings, but Freud believed that people are anything but rational, instead driven by selfish "animal" impulses. Freud alleged that these impulses are biological in origin, and they demand satisfaction even though they are part of what he called the unconscious mind.

∽

His was a hedonistic view, stating that we exist entirely to seek pleasure and avoid pain.

∽

Freud developed his theory through his treatment of typically mildly disordered patients, which eventually yielded the treatment approach he called psychoanalysis.

Some of Freud's ideas have survived, but much of his theorizing has been discounted. However, he is still regarded as one of the most influential figures in all of psychology, and he was the first to attempt a comprehensive theory of personality.

CLINICAL PSYCHOLOGY

CLINICAL PSYCHOLOGY studies and treats mental and behavioral disorders and typically deals with the more serious illnesses. Clinical psychology has become a significant focus within psychology in the United States.

ဏ

Clinical psychologists often specialize in working with people of different age ranges or who have specific disorders, and psychotherapy and psychological testing are a large part of the work they do.

ဏ

In 1896 at the University of Pennsylvania, **LIGHTNER WITMER**, a student of Wilhelm Wundt, established the world's first psychological clinic and originated the field of clinical psychology. Witmer started the first journal in the field in 1907, *The Psychological Clinic*, in which he coined the term *clinical psychology*.

ဏ

World War II provided a major impetus to the field as psychologists were called upon to treat returning service men suffering from shell shock.

ဏ

Although clinical psychology is rooted in experimentation and the scientific method, it has moved away from science despite strides made in complementary areas such as neuroimaging, molecular and behavioral genetics, and cognitive neuroscience.

∽

Research has shown that a number of psychological interventions are efficacious and cost-effective, important considerations in the face of rising healthcare costs. However, these therapies are not used as often as they could be because practitioners often value their personal and subjective clinical experiences more highly than scientific evidence.

EXTRACURRICULARS: DRAMA CLUB
Actor **KELSEY GRAMMER** holds the record for playing the same character on television for the most years. He played psychiatrist Dr. Frasier Crane for twenty years on *Cheers* and its spinoff *Frasier*.

SOPHOMORE YEAR: ECONOMICS

MICROECONOMICS

MICROECONOMICS focuses on the role individual consumers, households, and firms play in the economy.

∽

It looks at when customers purchase goods, and the price at which goods are sold.

∽

UTILITY is the benefit or satisfaction one might receive from an item or a good. The more benefit, the more consumers are willing to pay.

The amount of satisfaction one unit of a good will bring is known as **MARGINAL UTILITY**. The more a good is consumed, the lower the marginal utility.

The summation of marginal utilities is called **TOTAL UTILITY**. For example, with the first piece of cake, the marginal utility will be high. But when the sixth pieces comes along, the total utility will be low.

There is a method of measuring cost through identifying another alternative use of the money. The lost profit is called **OPPORTU-NITY COST**. For example, if you decide to eat out at an expensive restaurant instead of staying home and cooking, the opportunity cost is what that money could have been used for instead in the future.

When consumers or business buy or create goods, they are risking the chance of not buying or creating another good, which is their opportunity cost.

A **MARKET FAILURE** is any situation that will disturb the competitive market.

Market failures affect the pricing of a good. If a company has a monopoly on a good, it can raise prices without consequence since there is no other good like it on the market.

MACROECONOMICS

MACROECONOMICS is the study of economy or regional econo-
mies, focusing on what causes the economy to grow or fluctuate,
changes in employment or unemployment, performance of the international trade, and the result of economic politics.

⟾

Macroeconomists try to predict economic conditions to better pre-
pare governments, firms, and consumers for the future.

⟾

Macroeconomics is about trying to understand the bigger picture.

⟾

The most commonly used indicator on economic behavior is the
GROSS DOMESTIC PRODUCT (GDP), or total value of goods and
services produced in a year within a country.

⟾

The **GROSS NATIONAL PRODUCT (GNP)** is the total value of
goods and services produced by residents from a country even if they
are living abroad. Outsourcing and foreign firms within a country are
included in the GNP, but not the GDP.

⟾

INFLATION is the continual rise in prices of a good. As a result, the
value of the dollar does not remain the same.

⟾

FISCAL POLICY refers to government decisions pertaining to taxa-
tion and spending with the goal of economic growth.

The Federal Reserve System sets the **MONETARY POLICY**, or the regulation of interest rates and supply of money, to ensure sustainable growth.

SUPPLY AND DEMAND

One of the most fundamental concepts to understanding economics is **SUPPLY AND DEMAND**.

∽

SUPPLY pertains to how much of a good is available, while **DEMAND** pertains to how much of a good people want. The price of goods and services is a direct reflection of the intersection of these two. As prices of a good increase, the quantity of that good increases and vice versa. This is known as **THE LAW OF SUPPLY**.

∽

As the price of a good increases, the demand from the consumer will decrease and vice versa. This is known as the **LAW OF DEMAND**.

EXTRACURRICULARS: YEARBOOK
MOST LIKELY TO CREATE A NEW FIELD
In 1776, **ADAM SMITH** published *The Wealth of Nations*, which is considered the first work of modern economics. Smith, for his views on division of labor, productivity, and free markets, is often referred to as the "father" of modern economics.

∽

When supply and demand are equal, the economy is said to be in **EQUILIBRIUM**. The amount of a good supplied is equal to the amount of a good demanded.

Equilibrium cannot truly be achieved in the real marketplace. It is simply an economic theory.

DISEQUILIBRIUM is when the amount supplied does not equal the amount demanded at the definite price.

JUNIOR YEAR: SOCIOLOGY

INTRODUCTION TO SOCIOLOGY

SOCIOLOGY is a social science that studies human social behavior, societies, their interactions, and the processes that affect them.

Sociology is concerned with economic, political, social, and religious activity, and all parts of societies including communities, institutions, specific populations, and groups as defined by gender, age, or race.

Sociologists study social status and stratification, deviant or criminal behaviors, social movements, and revolution. Sociologists also attempt to determine how laws or rules govern human social behavior.

Because humans lack the instincts that direct the actions of most animals, people largely depend on social institutions to provide the norms that regulate human behavior. Sociology attempts to determine the role of these institutions, how they are established and dissolve, how they interact with each other, and how they gain or lose influence.

∽

Basic organizational structures include economic, educational, religious, and political institutions.

∽

Contemporary study of sociology combines an examination of classical theories and modern qualitative and quantitative methods.

HISTORY OF SOCIOLOGY

The history of sociology is connected very closely to philosophy, as many philosophers and political theorists, going back to the time of Plato, have considered broad social issues in their writings.

∽

AUGUSTE COMTE (1798–1857) was a French philosopher influential in the founding of sociology. Comte founded the school of philosophy known as **POSITIVISM**, which maintains that the only knowledge is scientific knowledge. He believed that sociology combines all the sciences and, through the methods of positivism, could achieve a society in which people lived in harmony and comfort.

∽

HERBERT SPENCER (1820–1903), an English sociologist and philosopher, believed in the natural basis of human action and, along with Charles Darwin, was an early supporter of the **THEORY OF EVOLUTION**. Spencer, however, believed that evolution was a progressive force directed toward good.

ÉMILE DURKHEIM (1858–1917), a French social scientist, is traditionally considered to be the "father" of sociology. He brought the scientific methodology of empirical research to the study of sociological theory and established sociology as an academic discipline.

MAX WEBER (1864–1920) was a German sociologist, economist, and political scientist. He developed an objective methodology for social science that considerably influenced twentieth-century sociologists. Weber argued for the role of belief systems, including religious values and ideologies, in shaping societies.

KARL MARX (1818–1883), the German social philosopher and socialist, was an important influence on sociological thought. Marx felt that the organization and development of society was economically motivated and class struggle the primary factor of social progress.

SOCIOLOGY IN AMERICA

GEORGE FITZHUGH (1806–1881) and **HENRY HUGHES** (1829–1862) offered a defense of slavery based on their belief that society needed a hierarchical structure of superiors and dependents. The Civil War put an end to this line of reasoning.

WILLIAM GRAHAM SUMNER (1840–1910) was an influential pioneer in the study of sociology. He advocated extreme **LAISSEZ-FAIRE ECONOMICS** and individual liberties, strongly opposing any government interference with free-market trade.

Sumner's sociological thought followed the same paths of **SELF-DETERMINATION**: the forces of competition eliminated poorly adapted individuals and preserved cultural soundness. He believed that the middle-class work ethic, thrift, and sobriety would lead to a wholesome, moral society.

Another important thought leader in sociological study was **LESTER FRANK WARD** (1841–1913), who developed the theory of **TELESIS**, which is the idea of planned social progress made possible by an active government. This type of society employed social scientists to provide a nationally organized education.

Ward believed that human intelligence rather than nature guided social evolution.

An early classic in the field of sociology was the series of **MIDDLE-TOWN** books authored by the husband and wife team of American sociologists **ROBERT STAUGHTON LYND** (1892–1970) and **HELEN MERRELL LYND** (1896–1982).

The first volume, *Middletown: A Study in Contemporary American Culture* (1929) was a treatise on social stratification in the community of Muncie, Indiana, using anthropological study techniques. They published a follow-up study in 1937, *Middletown in Transition: A Study in Cultural Conflicts*, which analyzed the social changes brought about by the Great Depression.

THEORIES IN SOCIOLOGY

CONFLICT THEORY emphasizes the importance of conflict in driving social change and draws upon the work of Karl Marx.

ꙮ

One conflict theorist was British sociologist **RALF DAHRENDORF** (1929–2009), who published *Class and Class Conflict in Industrial Society* in 1959. He went beyond Marx's narrow view that class is defined by property ownership and claimed that modern struggles are between those with authority and those without. Capitalism, changed from the times of Marx, has institutionalized conflict through the creation of unions, collective bargaining, the court system, and political debate.

ꙮ

STRUCTURAL FUNCTIONALISM was greatly influenced by the work of American sociologist **ROBERT K. MERTON** (1910–2003).

ꙮ

He attempted to explain the function of social structures as well as their dysfunctions and balances. Instead of analyzing society as a whole, Merton examined different social structures, such as groups, organizations, or communities. His published works include *Social Theory and Social Structure* (1949).

ꙮ

The study of symbolic interaction was begun by American social psychologist **GEORGE HERBERT MEAD** (1863–1931).

ꙮ

SYMBOLIC INTERACTION THEORY posits that the world people inhabit is built on the interpretation given to objects, and interpretations vary from one group to another. Even the way we look at ourselves is based on our interpretation of how others see us.

∽

Mead's work was further developed by American sociologist **HERBERT BLUMER** (1900–1987). He coined the term *symbolic interaction* and defined the three premises on which the theory is based:

1. Human beings act toward things, be they objects, people, institutions, or ideas, based on the meanings the things have for them
2. The meaning of such things derives from social interaction.
3. These meanings are handled in, and modified by, an individual's interpretive process.

EXTRACURRICULARS: STUDENT COUNCIL

Before becoming a U.S. senator, **DANIEL PATRICK MOYNIHAN** worked as a sociologist as the director of the then named Joint Center for Urban Studies of MIT and Harvard University. In 1965, while assistant secretary of labor, he released *The Negro Family: The Case for National Action* (also know as the Moynihan Report), which examined black poverty in America and called for government action on behalf of black families.

SENIOR YEAR: POLITICAL SCIENCE

DEMOCRACY AND THE CONSTITUTION

DEMOCRACY comes from the Greek word *demos* meaning "people." In democracies, people make legislative decisions.

FORMS OF DEMOCRACY:

- **DIRECT DEMOCRACY:** Citizens make decisions regarding policies and laws directly. In other words, all citizens vote on all issues.
- **REPRESENTATIVE DEMOCRACY:** Citizens vote for representatives who will govern them. This is the model used in the United States, which was formed as a republic, a type of representative democracy.
- **PARLIAMENTARY DEMOCRACY:** A form of representative democracy in which the dominant party within the legislature selects members of the government.

In the United States, the **CONSTITUTION** is the basis for the government. The document tells Americans what rights they have as citizens, and also serves as protection of those rights.

The **PREAMBLE** states the reasons for separating from England during the Revolutionary War. The seven articles that follow establish the three branches of government, allows states the right to carry out their own laws, and provides that the Constitution can change through amendments.

IMPORTANT AMENDMENTS TO KNOW:

- **FIRST AMENDMENT:** Freedom of speech, religion, the press, assembly, and the right to petition the government.
- **FIFTH AMENDMENT:** The right to due process.

- **THIRTEENTH AMENDMENT:** The abolition of slavery.
- **NINETEENTH AMENDMENT:** Women's right to vote.

ഗ

The Constitution also set up the **ELECTORAL COLLEGE** to officially elect the president. Each state has a certain number of electors, representative of its population (the number of representatives plus the two senators from each state). Citizens vote in the popular vote, but it is the electors who actually cast the votes to elect the president. Electors generally vote with the majority of their state, but are not required to.

ഗ

There is a great debate as to whether we need the Electoral College. In 2000, Al Gore won the popular vote, but George W. Bush won the Electoral College vote, showing that winning the majority of citizens' confidence did not matter.

OTHER FORMS OF GOVERNMENT

COMMUNISM is a philosophy based on the works of Karl Marx and Friedrich Engels, which called for an abolition of capitalism and private ownership. It is based on government control of labor, education, communication, transportation, agriculture, and factories, as well as an abolition of religion and the class system.

ഗ

North Korea, Cuba, and China are all currently communist countries.

ഗ

The type of government in which one individual possesses all political power, either nominally, or absolutely, is known as a **MONARCHY**. Generally, in a hereditary monarchy, the crown is passed down through family.

Brunei, Oman, Qatar, Saudi Arabia, Swaziland, and Vatican City are ruled by absolute monarchs, but there are forty-four other monarchical nations, including the United Kingdom and Spain.

A government where the political power rests in the hands of a small group of people, generally those who are distinguished by royalty, wealth, or military strength is known as an **OLIGARCHY**.

According to some, modern democracies—including the United States—should be considered oligarchies.

TOTALITARIANISM is a government run by a dictator or party with absolute control over the people and the land. There is often an emphasis on nationalism, achieved through oppressive military regimes and propaganda.

Hitler, Stalin, and Mussolini were all examples of totalitarian dictators. Today, China and North Korea are still ruled in this way.

EXTRACURRICULARS: NEWSPAPER
COLD WAR ENDS AS USSR DISSOLVES

In December 1991, Soviet president Mikhail Gorbachev resigned from office, and turned over leadership of the new Russian Federation to Boris Yeltsin. In doing so, the communist state of the USSR was officially dissolved, making way for fifteen new independent nations, and giving way to democracy in the region.

FINAL EXAM

IT'S TIME TO FIND OUT if you're at the head of the class, or if you need to go back to school . . . again. Twenty multiple choice questions follow based on the ten classes you just completed. Try to test you knowledge on the honor system, without scanning back through the chapters. You'll find the answers and your scoring criteria at the end. Good luck!

1. Which of the following is **NOT** a part of speech?
   A. Noun
   B. Verb
   C. Semicolon
   D. Adjective

2. Who of the following authors could be described as a transcendentalist?
   A. Stephen King
   B. Virginia Woolf
   C. William Shakespeare
   D. Henry David Thoreau

3. Pluto can be described as a(n):
   A. Asteroid
   B. Dwarf planet
   C. Galaxy
   D. Solar system

4. What is the smallest unit of life in an organism's body?
   A. DNA
   B. Mitosis
   C. Cell
   D. RNA

5. What is the capital of Canada?
   A. Ottawa
   B. Washington
   C. Toronto
   D. Nunavut

6. Where is the country of Fiji located?
   A. Asia
   B. Africa
   C. South America
   D. Oceania

7. Which of the following did the Mesopotamians **NOT** develop?
   A. Irrigation methods
   B. The wheel
   C. Sails to harness wind energy
   D. Copper

8. The assassination of Archduke Franz Ferdinand was the impetus for which major world event?
   A. World War I
   B. World War II
   C. American Revolution
   D. War on Terror

9. The game "tsu chu" is known as what today?
   A. Baseball
   B. Soccer
   C. Hockey
   D. Tennis

10. Which baseball player had the nickname "the Sultan of Swat"?
    A. Jackie Robinson
    B. Pete Rose
    C. Babe Ruth
    D. Joe DiMaggio

11. In the algebraic expression $8x^3$, 8 represents the:
    A. Coefficient
    B. Variable
    C. Exponent
    D. Logarithm

12. Which is an example of a mathematical constant?
    A. x
    B. $2x^3$
    C. π
    D. y

13. Which philosopher, who never wrote a single word for posterity, is known as the single most important in history?
    A. Socrates
    B. Aristotle
    C. Sartre
    D. Marx

14. Who said: "I think, therefore I am"?
    A. David Hume
    B. René Descartes
    C. Sir Isaac Newton
    D. Immanuel Kant

15. Which of the following is known as a Romance language?
    A. Dutch
    B. Russian
    C. Portuguese
    D. Chinese

16. Which of the following is a language spoken in China?
    A. Mandarin
    B. Cantonese
    C. All of the above
    D. None of the above

17. Which artist is **NOT** best known for his work during the High Renaissance?
    A. Donatello
    B. Leonardo da Vinci
    C. Michelangelo
    D. Raphael

18. The art of Claude Monet can be described as:
    A. Pop art
    B. Cubism
    C. Impressionist
    D. Expressionist

19. When the amount of a good supplied in the marketplace is equal to the amount of a good demanded, it is known as:
    A. Microeconomics
    B. Equilibrium
    C. Disequilibrium
    D. Inflation

20. A government whose power rests in the hands of a small group of people is known as a(n):
    A. Oligarchy
    B. Monarchy
    C. Totalitarian dictatorship
    D. Direct democracy

ANSWER KEY

1-C, 2-D, 3-B, 4-C, 5-A, 6-D, 7-D, 8-A, 9-B, 10-C, 11-A, 12-C, 13-A, 14-B, 15-C, 16-C, 17-A, 18-C, 19-B, 20-A

Give yourself one point for each correct answer, and see how you did:

0–6 POINTS—
HELD BACK:
Your trip back to school was not a success. We recommend summer school, or you may have to repeat high school—again!

7–13 POINTS—
RIGHT DOWN THE MIDDLE:
You only have to pass to graduate, so congratulations on your perfectly average score. Look forward to a life in middle management.

14–20 POINTS—
SUMMA CUM LAUDE:
You're at the top of your class, graduate, and your future is looking bright. You should be receiving calls any minute now from the Ivy League, the *Fortune* 500, and maybe even the president.

INDEX